Unveiling the Unknown:
A History of Data Science's Foundational Moments

Sana

Contents

Part I.

Introduction

1. Introduction

1.1. Statistical vs. Machine Learning

In the 1960s the scientific discipline known as data science or data analysis emerged [59]. In the 1920s and 1930s, Fisher's paradigm on the fundamental question:

> "What must one know a priori about an unknown functional dependency in order to estimate it on the basis of observations?"

gave the restricted answer - one must know almost everything. Between 1960 and 1980 a new paradigm rose.

> "It was shown that in order to estimate dependency from the data, it is sufficient to know some general properties of the set of functions to which the unknown dependency belongs." [61]

According to Vapnik [61] four discoveries in the 1960s led to the new theory:

i) Discovery of regularization principles for solving ill-posed problems by Tikhonov, Ivanov and Phillips.

ii) Discovery of nonparametric statistics by Parzen, Rosenblatt and Chentsov.

iii) Discovery of the law of large numbers in functional space and its relation to the learning processes by Vapnik and Chervonenkis.

iv) Discovery of algorithmic complexity and its relation to inductive inference by Kolmogorov, Solomonoff and Chaitin.

From this new theory two cultures emerged, statistical and machine learning [12]. Statistical learning concerns with interpretable models and inference of covariates. Machine learning came up with new powerful algorithms in the 1980s, namely neural networks and decision trees. In statistical learning the data is considered as sampled realizations of random variables. It uses major concepts such as probability, significance and tests. In machine learning predictive power is the main concern. The variables are entities providing information. It is hard to reveal the knowledge the algorithm gains because of its complexity. Therefore machine learning methods are often called black-boxes. But there is a lot of ongoing research in understanding and interpreting the processes [25, 47, 44]. And this research is needed because it is still not understood when a method may fail and, even worse, it is not even apparent if the method gives a correct or incorrect result [24]. The challenge for the future seems to be to somehow combine these two cultures in order to get powerful, instructive methods.

1.2. Objective of book

The objective of this book is the enhancement of logistic regression for prospectivity model-ing. Although the proposed technique can also be applied to data arising in other fields, the main emphasis lies in the setting of prospectivity modeling. This comprises a setting with large amount of data, i.e. millions or even billions of samples, and a target event that is rare, i.e. only 0.1% of the examples are positive. Logistic regression is well understood and has a firm statistical foundation. It can be considered to be a statistical method being on the cusp of machine learning. The fitting of a logistic regression model is furthermore computational cheap. The disadvantage of only being a linear predictor can be overcome with some adjustments and extensions. This makes logistic regression more powerful. Its relationship to neural networks is shown and helps to guide the enhancement in order to come close to the predictive power of a neural network. It furthermore helps to link logistic regression to neural networks and guides the understanding of the latter. A well fitted logistic regression model has the advantage of providing an explicit model to the researcher that can be used to gain knowledge and understanding of the underlying problem.

1.3. Organization of The book

The book is divided into four parts. Following this introduction, part two provides the reader with background information on the algorithms and concepts we use. Part three puts these things together and contains the proposed method with some adaption. It also shows the performance on artificial and real world datasets. This includes data from mineral prospectivity modeling, i.e. gold mineralisation, in Ghana. The final part states the conclusions drawn from this research.

1.4. Notation

This is a description of the mathematical notation used in this book. Lowercase letters refer to scalar variables. Vectors are displayed using bold lowercase letters. A vector is always con-sidered to be a column vector. A matrix is displayed in uppercase bold letters. Mathematical spaces as well as the expectation and variance are displayed using blackboard bold.

Part II.

Background

2. Prospectivity Modeling

The objective of prospectivity modeling in geoscience is to predict locations where a target event, e.g., a gold mineralisation, is present. Or more specifically the conditional probability of the occurrence of the target given the data. This conditional probability is dependent on some covariates that can be favorable or unfavorable for the indicator target variable. Although a lot of methods for tackling this problem would be labeled "data driven", expert knowledge is still a key ingredient for successful predictions. The understanding of the target variable in terms of cause and effect is needed to carefully select the covariates that induce the target, i.e., that capture geological, geophysical, geochemical and other features of the region. Conceptual large scale models for describing the genetic processes of mineralisations in terms of cause and effect are known as mineral system approach [18, 64, 3, 41, 55]. The geological data is either available in digital two dimensional or three dimensional form, namely as geological map images or geological models in raster mode, respectively. So the covariates and data are supported by pixels (2D) or voxels (3D). Another possibility is the description of the data using polygons or polyhedrons. In order to establish a mathematical model that is able to predict future occurrences of the studied target, a training region is needed. The modeling assumption regarding this training region is perfect knowledge, meaning that every occurrence of the target within this region is known. The data with a given spatial resolution which is adequate for sound economic-ecologic decisions can then be used to fit a model and estimate its parameters. The spatial resolution of the model is again a user decision that should be guided by knowledge and experience. It is furthermore dependent on the possibilities and technical restriction of data acquisition. Unfortunately, different spatial resolutions will lead to different prospectivity models. Even worse, it was shown that different spatial resolution may lead to inconsistent prospectivity models [9]. This is a fact one needs to be aware of and a fitted model should be applied only to unseen data in the same spatial resolution. Furthermore, except for spatial point processes [7], the methods described here do not consider spatial dependency. Thus although there is of course a relationship between two datapoints that geological lie close to each other, the methods do not consider it. This means one could rearrange all datapoints and all predictions for every datapoint would still be the same.

Different methods are known to establish a model. A very popular method in geoscience is the weights of evidence (WoE) approach [26, 1]. It uses Bayes' theorem and the assumption of joint conditional independence of all indicator covariates given the target, such that the model parameters can be estimated through mere counting. However, a violation of the conditional independence assumptions corrupts the model. Not only in the sense that the estimated conditional probabilities are wrong, but also their rank transform [50]. This means the location of the maximum conditional probability might change. As a remedy one could test the indicator covariates for joint conditional independence [51]. Furthermore, attempts to relax the modeling assumption are made [21, 52, 14, 54]. The restriction to indicator covariates limits the application of WoE. Another method is compositional regression [3], which uses log-ratio transforms to express the target as ratios of components.

The main approach considered in this book is logistic regression [30, 32], which is the canonical generalization of WoE. There are several other methods and an overview of current methods for prospectivity modeling covering statistical learning as well as machine learning is given in [53].

3. Linear Regression

Linear regression is used to describe the relation between some predictor variables $x_i, i = 1, \ldots m$ and a target or outcome variable y. The model has the form

$$f(\boldsymbol{x}, \boldsymbol{\beta}) = \beta_0 + \beta_1 x_1 + \cdots + \beta_m x_m \tag{3.1}$$

where the vector $\boldsymbol{\beta}$ contains the parameters that need to be estimated, with β_0 being the intercept or offset. For convenience we assume an additional variable x_0 which is set to $x_0 \equiv 1$. The model can then be written in short form as

$$f(\boldsymbol{x}, \boldsymbol{\beta}) = \boldsymbol{\beta}^\top \boldsymbol{x}. \tag{3.2}$$

Due to measurement errors or other random processes the target variable does not correspond to the model perfectly. Therefore we use a statistical model that accounts for this randomness, i.e.

$$y = f(\boldsymbol{x}, \boldsymbol{\beta}) + \epsilon, \tag{3.3}$$

where ϵ is a normally distributed error term with zero mean and unknown variance σ^2 which is independent of $\boldsymbol{x}$. Hence the conditional expected value of the model is

$$\begin{aligned} \mathbb{E}(y|\boldsymbol{x}) &= f(\boldsymbol{x}, \boldsymbol{\beta}) + \mathbb{E}(\epsilon) \tag{3.4}\\ &= f(\boldsymbol{x}, \boldsymbol{\beta}) \tag{3.5} \end{aligned}$$

Consider now a data matrix $\boldsymbol{X} \in \mathbb{R}^{n \times m+1}$ containing n experiments. Each experiment is described by m variables and the intercept. Furthermore let $\boldsymbol{y} \in \mathbb{R}^n$ be the vector containing the outcome of each experiment. The task is now to find the best approximation of the true parameters $\boldsymbol{\beta}$ such that equation (3.3) is optimal in some sense for the given data. Using the least squares method the objective to minimize is the residual sum of squares (RSS), defined as

$$\begin{aligned} \text{RSS}(\boldsymbol{\beta}) &= \sum_{i=1}^{n}(y_i - \boldsymbol{\beta}^\top \boldsymbol{x}_i)^2 \\ &= (\boldsymbol{y} - \boldsymbol{\beta}^\top \boldsymbol{x})^\top (\boldsymbol{y} - \boldsymbol{\beta}^\top \boldsymbol{x}) \tag{3.6} \end{aligned}$$

where $\boldsymbol{x}_i$ denotes the i-th experiment (i-th row) of $\boldsymbol{X}$ and $\boldsymbol{\beta}$ are the parameters that need to be adjusted. In order to find the least squares estimator (LSE) $\hat{\boldsymbol{\beta}}$ one needs to minimize equation (3.6), i.e.

$$\hat{\boldsymbol{\beta}} = \min_{\boldsymbol{\beta}} \text{RSS}(\boldsymbol{\beta}). \tag{3.7}$$

This is achieved by computing partial derivatives of all $\tilde{\beta}_i, i = 0, \ldots, m$ and setting them to zero. This gives the score equation $\boldsymbol{X}^\top(\boldsymbol{X}\boldsymbol{\beta} - \boldsymbol{y}) = 0$. Hence the LSE is given by

$$\hat{\boldsymbol{\beta}} = (\boldsymbol{X}^\top \boldsymbol{X})^{-1} \boldsymbol{X}^\top \boldsymbol{y}. \tag{3.8}$$

Since the expectation of $\hat{\boldsymbol{\beta}}$ is equal to $\boldsymbol{\beta}$ it is an unbiased estimator. The covariance matrix is given by $\text{cov}(\hat{\boldsymbol{\beta}}) = \sigma^{-2}(\boldsymbol{X}^\top \boldsymbol{X})^{-1}$ [45].

A more general approach is the maximum likelihood method. Since the samples are independent and identical distributed the likelihood function is given as

$$L(\boldsymbol{y}, \boldsymbol{X}, \boldsymbol{\beta}, \sigma^2) = P(y_1 | \boldsymbol{x}_1, \boldsymbol{\beta}, \sigma^2) \cdot \cdots \cdot P(y_n | \boldsymbol{x}_n, \boldsymbol{\beta}, \sigma^2)$$

$$= (2\pi\sigma^2)^{-\frac{n}{2}} \prod_{i=1}^{n} \exp\left(-\frac{1}{2\sigma^2} (y_i - \boldsymbol{\beta}^\top \boldsymbol{x}_i)^2 \right) \tag{3.9}$$

This function is maximized over $\boldsymbol{\beta}$ to give the maximum likelihood estimate (MLE) . Since we are only interested into the location of the maximum and not the value of the maximum itself we can use the log-transform of equation (3.9). Additionally ignoring constant terms results in

$$\ln L(\boldsymbol{y}, \boldsymbol{X}, \boldsymbol{\beta}) = \sum_{i=1}^{n} -(y_i - \boldsymbol{\beta}^\top \boldsymbol{x}_i)^2$$

$$= -(\boldsymbol{y} - \boldsymbol{\beta}^\top \boldsymbol{X})^\top (\boldsymbol{y} - \boldsymbol{\beta}^\top \boldsymbol{X}). \tag{3.10}$$

Minimizing the negative of (3.10) gives the exact same formulation as the RSS formula (3.6). In the case where the variance of the error is different but known for every sample one can use the diagonal matrix $\boldsymbol{W} = \mathrm{diag}(\sigma_i^2), i = 1, \ldots, n$, to standardize unequal variances. This gives the new score equations $\boldsymbol{X}^\top \boldsymbol{W}(\boldsymbol{X}\boldsymbol{\beta} - \boldsymbol{y}) = 0$ and thus the weighted least square estimator is

$$\hat{\boldsymbol{\beta}} = (\boldsymbol{X}^\top \boldsymbol{W} \boldsymbol{X})^{-1} \boldsymbol{X}^\top \boldsymbol{W} \boldsymbol{y}. \tag{3.11}$$

4. Logistic Regression

4.1. Logistic Regression Model

The logistic regression model is a well known method for classification in case of a dichotomous outcome variable. A comprehensive introduction to the topic is given by Hosmer and Lemeshow [32]. Similar to linear regression the aim of logistic regression is to model the relation between a target variable and one or more predictor variables. Logistic regression is a special case of a generalized linear model (GLM). These models come into play when there is no linear relationship between the outcome and the predictor variables. Consider the example data given in Figure 4.1(a). The dichotomous target variable y is plot against one explanatory predictor variable x. When fitting a linear model, the estimates range over the whole axis of

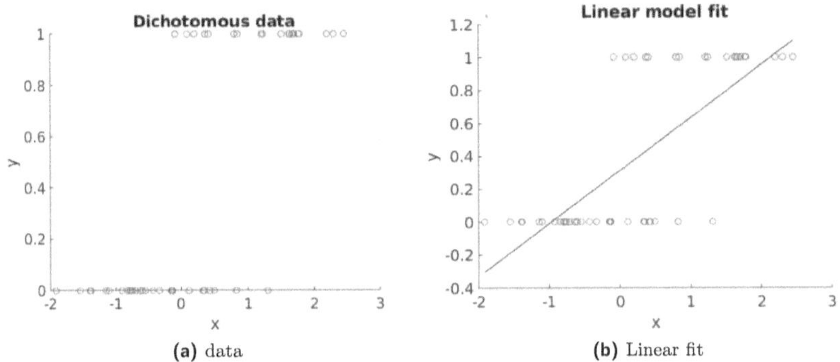

(a) data   (b) Linear fit

Fig. 4.1.: (a) Scatterplot of a binary outcome variable y depending on one normally distributed predictor variable x for 50 values. (b) Linear fit to the data.

real numbers although in reality it only can become zero or one; see Figure 4.1(b). Hence with a dichotomous outcome variable the conditional expectation must be greater than zero and smaller than one. The percentage of values $y = 1$ in an interval $[x_0, x_1]$ continually increases as the interval is shifted to the right. The percentage starts at zero and finally reaches one; see Figure 4.2(a). This emerging curve is called a sigmoid curve and it resembles a plot of a cumulative distribution of a continuous random variable. The idea to use a known cumulative distribution function for modeling $\mathbb{E}(y|\boldsymbol{x})$ in the case when y is a dichotomous variable seems obvious. There are several distribution functions that can be used but the most popular is the logistic distribution. It is easy to use, flexible, and the the model parameters provide meaningful estimates of effects [32].

When the logistic distribution is used the conditional mean is represented with $\mu(\boldsymbol{x}) = \mathbb{E}(y|\boldsymbol{x})$ using the logistic function

$$\mu(\boldsymbol{x}) = \frac{\exp(\boldsymbol{\beta}^\top \boldsymbol{x})}{1 + \exp(\boldsymbol{\beta}^\top \boldsymbol{x})} \tag{4.1}$$

with $\boldsymbol{\beta} = (\beta_0, \ldots, \beta_m)$ being the parameter vector that needs to be estimated. To emphasize the dependency of the logistic function on the parameters and the data we will denote it

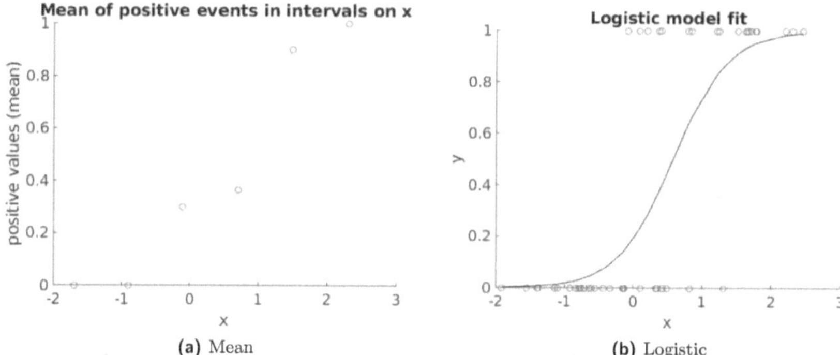

(a) Mean

(b) Logistic

Fig. 4.2.: Scatterplot of a binary outcome variable y depending on one normally distributed explanatory variable x for 50 values.

with $\mu(\boldsymbol{x}, \boldsymbol{\beta})$. The fitted logistic function for the example data can be seen in Figure 4.2(b). It fulfills the property that its output is between zero and one. Furthermore it can be seen that the change per unit in x becomes smaller as the conditional mean approaches zero or one. The conditional expectation of this model is equivalent to the conditional probability:

$$\mathbb{E}(y|\boldsymbol{x}) = 1 \cdot P(y = 1|\boldsymbol{x}) + 0 \cdot P(y = 0|\boldsymbol{x}) = P(y = 1|\boldsymbol{x}). \tag{4.2}$$

The logistic regression model is then defined as

$$y = \mu(\boldsymbol{x}, \boldsymbol{\beta}) + \epsilon. \tag{4.3}$$

A central transformation of $\mu(\boldsymbol{x}, \boldsymbol{\beta})$ is its inverse $g(\mu)$ which is called the logit transformation. It is defined, in terms of $\mu(\boldsymbol{x}, \boldsymbol{\beta})$, as

$$g(\mu) = \text{logit}(\mu(\boldsymbol{x}, \boldsymbol{\beta})) = \ln \frac{\mu(\boldsymbol{x}, \boldsymbol{\beta})}{1 - \mu(\boldsymbol{x}, \boldsymbol{\beta})} = \boldsymbol{\beta}^\top \boldsymbol{x}. \tag{4.4}$$

Since $\mu(\boldsymbol{x}, \boldsymbol{\beta}) = P(y|\boldsymbol{x})$ this is the same as the logarithm of the odds. The logit transformation is linear in its parameters. Thus it has many desirable properties of a linear regression model. However, the error in the logistic regression model (4.3) is not normally distributed as it was in the linear regression model. It can only assume two possible values. If $y = 1$ we have $\epsilon = 1 - \mu(\boldsymbol{x}, \boldsymbol{\beta})$ with probability $\mu(\boldsymbol{x}, \boldsymbol{\beta})$. If $y = 0$ we have $\epsilon = -\mu(\boldsymbol{x}, \boldsymbol{\beta})$ with probability $1 - \mu(\boldsymbol{x}, \boldsymbol{\beta})$. Thus the error ϵ has a distribution with mean zero and variance $\mu(\boldsymbol{x}, \boldsymbol{\beta})(1 - \mu(\boldsymbol{x}, \boldsymbol{\beta}))$. The error follows a binomial distribution. Hence the conditional distribution of the outcome variable y follows a binomial distribution. As shown in (4.2) its conditional probability is given by the conditional mean $\mu(\boldsymbol{x}, \boldsymbol{\beta})$.

In the following, we assume to have n datapoints and m predictor variables which are also called covariates or features. They are contained in the data matrix $\boldsymbol{X} \in \mathbb{R}^{n \times m+1}$ where the additional covariate describes the intercept $\boldsymbol{x}_0$, a column only consisting of ones, similar as in linear regression. Every row in the data matrix $\boldsymbol{X}$ describes an experiment. Every experiment has an outcome or target, which is described by a variable $y \in \{0, 1\}$. The vector of all outcomes of every experiment is $\boldsymbol{y} \in \{0, 1\}^n$

We emphasize that LR is a linear classifier. It can be thought of as finding a hyperplane to separate the two classes of the target event. This can often be a limitation, and we will address this problem later.

4.2. Maximum Likelihood Estimation

As seen in section 3, a general method for determining the parameter vector is called maximum likelihood estimation. This method gives an estimation of the parameter that maximizes the probability to get the observed data. To model the probability of the observed data as a function of the parameter β one uses the likelihood function. Recall that the outcome y is a Bernoulli random variable. The conditional mean $\mu(x, \beta)$ describes the conditional probability to obtain $y = 1$ given the data x. Likewise the conditional probability to obtain $y = 0$ given the data x is described by $1 - \mu(x, \beta)$. To summarize, the conditional probability for the i-th experiment and outcome in the dataset X, i.e. the conditional probability of y_i, can be computed by

$$P(y_i|x_i, \beta) = \begin{cases} \mu(x_i, \beta) & \text{if } y_i = 1, \\ 1 - \mu(x_i, \beta) & \text{if } y_i = 0, \end{cases} \tag{4.5}$$
$$= \mu(x_i, \beta)^{y_i}(1 - \mu(x_i, \beta))^{1-y_i}, \qquad i = 1, \ldots, n.$$

Because we assume the experiments to be independent the likelihood function is simply the product of all probabilities in (4.5):

$$l(\beta) = \prod_{i=1}^{n} \mu(x_i, \beta)^{y_i}(1 - \mu(x_i, \beta))^{1-y_i}. \tag{4.6}$$

The best estimation of β for the model (4.3) is the one that maximizes the likelihood function (4.6). The log-likelihood of the data X, y under the LR model with parameters β is

$$L(\beta) = \ln l(\beta) = \sum_{i=1}^{n} \Big(y_i \ln(\mu(x_i, \beta)) + (1 - y_i) \ln(1 - \mu(x_i, \beta)) \Big). \tag{4.7}$$

For computations the logarithm of the likelihood is used since the product is replaced by a sum, which is easier to handle. The location of the maximum does not change, so maximizing the log-likelihood is equivalent to maximizing the likelihood. Since the log-likelihood is nonlinear in β it cannot be solved analytically. Therefore numerical methods are used to find the maximum likelihood estimation (MLE) $\hat{\beta}$. Recall that LR is a member of the family of generalized linear models. The loss function for that type of model is a scaled likelihood ratio and is called the deviance. It is defined as

$$D = -2 \ln \left(\frac{l_{fit}}{l_{sat}} \right) \phi \tag{4.8}$$

where l_{fit} is the likelihood value of the fitted model, l_{sat} is the likelihood of the saturated model, and ϕ is the dispersion parameter, which is 1 in the logistic regression model [42]. For logistic regression with binary outcomes the likelihood of the saturated model is simply one and the deviance becomes [36]

$$D = -2 \ln l_{fit} = -2 \ln l(\beta) = -2L(\beta)$$
$$= -2 \sum_{i=1}^{n} \Big(y_i \ln(\mu(x_i, \beta)) + (1 - y_i)(1 - \mu(x_i, \beta)) \Big). \tag{4.9}$$

So maximizing the likelihood function is equivalent to minimizing the deviance, i.e. it results in the same estimation for the parameters.

4.3. Statistical Measures

In this section, we introduce some statistical measures that are used within this work. As already mentioned earlier a main advantage of logistic regression is its profound statistical foundation providing a lot of useful statistical measures.

4.3.1. Likelihood Ratio Test

The likelihood ratio test assesses the significance of a predictor variable by comparing the value of the deviance D of the model with and without the variable, i.e.

$$G = D(\text{model without the variable}) - D(\text{model with the variable}).$$

This can also be expressed in the form [32]

$$G = -2\ln\left[\frac{(\text{likelihood of the fitted model without the variable})}{(\text{likelihood of the fitted model with the variable})}\right]. \tag{4.10}$$

Under the hypothesis that the variable under consideration is zero the statistic G follows a chi-square distribution with one degree of freedom. In order to test for the significance of that variable one would compute the probability (p-value) that the chi-squared distribution with one degree of freedom, i.e. $\chi^2(1)$, takes a value greater than G, i.e. $p = P[\chi^2(1) > G]$.

In the case of an elimination of k variables from the initial model the statistic G follows a chi-square distribution with k degrees of freedom. If this p-value is smaller than a predefined threshold (usually $\alpha = 0.05$) the variable is considered to be significant for the model.

4.3.2. Wald statistic

The Wald statistic tests for the same null hypothesis as the likelihood ratio test, namely that the respective parameter equals zero. Then the ratio of the parameter of interest divided by its standard error follows a standard normal distribution, i.e.

$$W = \frac{\hat{\beta}}{\widehat{se}(\hat{\beta})} \sim \mathcal{N}(0,1) \tag{4.11}$$

The two-tailed p-value is then calculated as

$$p = P(|z| > W), \tag{4.12}$$

where z is a random variable following the standard normal distribution [32]. Similarly to the likelihood ration test the variable can be assumed to be significant if its p-value is smaller than a threshold. It is worth mentioning that the square of the Wald statistic follows a chi-square distribution with one degree of freedom. Thus one has $\sqrt{G} \approx W$.

4.3.3. Kullback-Leibler (K-L) Distance

The K-L distance or K-L information is an information measure derived by [37] in 1951. It can measure the distance of models f, g in the sense of the information that is lost when a model g is used to approximate f. It is defined as

$$I(f,g) = \int f(x) \log\left(\frac{f(x)}{g(x|\beta)}\right) dx, \tag{4.13}$$

where the integral is usually multi-dimensional and the logarithm denotes the natural logarithm. Speaking heuristically, $I(f,g)$ is the distance from g to f. The K-L distance is not symmetric, i.e. the distance from g to f is different from the distance from f to g. The K-L distance is a fundamental quality in information theory [4] as it is the basis for model selection in connection with likelihood inference. It is always greater equal to zero and is zero if and only if f and g are identical (i.e. $I(f,g) = 0 \Leftrightarrow f(x) = g(x)$). In the context of model selection one considers f as the truth or ground truth and g as a model that approximates that ground truth. This enables the use for model selection since f does not need to be known anymore [13]. This follows from the fact that we can write $I(f,g)$ equivalently as

$$I(f,g) = \int f(x)\log((f(x))dx - \int f(x)\log(g(x|\beta))dx.$$

Both terms on the right are statistical expectations with respect to f, giving

$$I(f,g) = \mathbb{E}_f[\log(f(x))] - \mathbb{E}_f[\log(g(x|\beta))]$$

The first term on the right is a constant C which cannot be estimated without knowing f. However, the calculation of a relative distance between f and g is possible, i.e.

$$I(f,g) - C = -\mathbb{E}_f[\log(g(x|\beta))].$$

This in turn enables the comparison of two models g_1 and g_2 for which one is the better approximation of f. Assume g_1 is the better model, this gives

$$I(f,g_1) < I(f,g_2)$$
$$I(f,g_1) - C < I(f,g_2) - C$$
$$-\mathbb{E}_f[\log(g_1(x|\beta))] < -\mathbb{E}_f[\log(g_2(x|\beta))].$$

Moreover, it is possible to determine how much better g_1 is than g_2 using $I(f,g_2) - I(f,g_1) = -\mathbb{E}_f[\log(g_2(x|\beta))] + \mathbb{E}_f[\log(g_1(x|\beta))]$. Note that without knowing C there is no information how well g_1 approximates f. Furthermore, the theory only holds when the parameter β is known, which is not the case in real world examples. Using it for estimated model parameters was proposed first by Akaike, see next subsection.

4.3.4. Akaike's Information Criterion (AIC)

Akaike proposed the use of K-L distance as basis for model selection [4]. For a parametric model there is in fact a unique value of β for which the corresponding model g minimizes the K-L distance $I(f,g)$. Denote this value $\bar{\beta}$. If g would be the K-L best model (which we do not know) then the MLE $\hat{\beta}$ would estimate $\bar{\beta}$. Having only the estimate $\hat{\beta}$ changes the model selection criterion to minimizing the expected estimated K-L distance $\mathbb{E}_y\mathbb{E}_x[\log(g(x|\beta(y)))]$ instead of the known K-L distance over a set of models considered. Akaike showed in [4] that estimating this relative expected K-L distance using the maximized log-likelihood for each model g_i is biased upwards. He found that the bias is approximately equal to the number of variables k in the model. Hence an unbiased estimator for the relative expected K-L distance is (multiplication by "-2" because of historical reason) [13]

$$\text{AIC} = -2L(\hat{\beta}) + 2k, \tag{4.14}$$

The AIC measures combines the goodness-of-fit and the complexity of a model, i.e. it penalizes models with larger complexity. However, if all models are poor, the AIC will still select the best model which might be still very poor in an absolute sense. Hence some kind of test on unseen data should be applied to assess the quality of the model.

The AIC also motivated the use of other penalty terms than $2k$. However, it is important that the penalty term in (4.14) is not chosen randomly but ensures an unbiased estimate of the relative expected K-L distance. The next subsection introduces another information criterion with a different penalty term.

4.3.5. Bayes' Information Criterion (BIC)

The BIC is similar to the AIC a measure for comparing models with different number of parameters and is defined as

$$BIC = -2L(\hat{\beta}) + \ln(n)k \tag{4.15}$$

with L and k being the same as in the definition of the AIC and n being the sample size. Although the AIC and BIC only differ in the penalty term, their derivation is quite different. As stated above the AIC finds the model that minimizes the K-L distance the the true model. The derivation of BIC is described in [13]. We state a short version of the derivation. The BIC is an approximation of the marginal probability of the data given as

$$\int \left[\prod_{i=1}^{n} g(\boldsymbol{x}_i|\boldsymbol{\beta}) \right] \pi(\boldsymbol{\beta})d\boldsymbol{\beta},$$

where $\pi(\boldsymbol{\beta})$ is the prior on the parameters $\boldsymbol{\beta}$. Considered as function of $\boldsymbol{\beta}$, the product under the integral is the likelihood. Hence it can be written as

$$\int \left[L(\boldsymbol{\beta}|\boldsymbol{X}, g) \right] \pi(\boldsymbol{\beta})d\boldsymbol{\beta}.$$

With increasing sample size and under some general regularity conditions one can approximate the likelihood near the MLE $\hat{\beta}$ as

$$L(\boldsymbol{\beta}|\boldsymbol{X}, g) = L(\hat{\beta}|\boldsymbol{X}, g) \exp(-\frac{1}{2}(\boldsymbol{\beta} - \hat{\beta})\mathbb{V}(\hat{\beta})^{-1}(\boldsymbol{\beta} - \hat{\beta})),$$

with $\mathbb{V}(\hat{\beta})$ being the estimated variance-covariance matrix of the MLE. The likelihood can be taken out of the integral and the remaining exponential function part can be evaluated. Taking -2 times the log of this approximation and dropping two terms that are asymptotically dominated by the term of order $\log(n)$ results in

$$-2\log(L(\boldsymbol{\beta}|\boldsymbol{X}, g)) + k\log(n).$$

Although the BIC is said to find the true model there is no mathematical evidence that the true model needs to be in the set of models. Comparing the second terms in AIC and BIC shows that the BIC penalizes the number of parameters more as soon as the sample size exceeds eight ($\ln(8) \approx 2.08$). So overall the BIC will select models that are greedier regarding the number of parameters.

4.4. Regularization

Maximizing the maximum-likelihood function for logistic regression may fail sometimes. Furthermore, correlation in the covariates may lead to large parameter estimates. Even worse, since most methods for estimating $\hat{\beta}$ are iterative, correlations may allow unbounded growth of the parameters and hence these methods may fail to converge. Another problem occurs if the data used for training is complete or quasi-complete separable. Then there exists no solution for the optimization problem [5]. Complete separation occurs if the outcome variable y can be perfectly predicted by one or more covariates. So for some covariate p there is a value t with $y_i = 1$ if $x_{ip} \geq t$ and $y_i = 0$ if $x_{ip} < t$ for $i = 1, \ldots, n$. As a consequence, the value β_p of the slope in this covariate would be chosen to be as large as possible. Since there is no upper bound for the parameter it would grow to infinity. Likewise quasi-complete separation occurs in the same setting as complete separation with the difference that at least one sample for each class has the value t, i.e. there exist at least two samples l, k with $y_k = 1$ and $y_l = 0$

for $x_{kp} = t$ and $x_{lp} = t$, respectively. The resulting problem is the same as with complete separation.

Another problem may be over-fitting. The MLE may be the best solution for the data it was trained on but may yield poor predictions on unseen data. All these problems can be tackled using regularization. This is realized by subtracting a term $R(\boldsymbol{\beta})$ from the log-likelihood so the regularized log-likelihood is given as

$$L(\boldsymbol{\beta}) = \sum_{i=1}^{n}(y_i \ln \mu(\boldsymbol{x}_i, \boldsymbol{\beta}) + (1 - y_i)\ln(1 - \mu(\boldsymbol{x}_i, \boldsymbol{\beta})) - R(\boldsymbol{\beta}). \tag{4.16}$$

Regularization has different possible interpretations. On the one hand the numerical point of view, where regularization is used to assure the existence of a solution or to deal with the singularity of the Hessian. On the other hand it corresponds to assuming a prior distribution of the parameters. This will be explained in more detail in the next subsections. There are a lot of different choices for the regularization term $R(\boldsymbol{\beta})$. We will introduce two different types that are probably used the most.

4.4.1. L_1-Regularization

L_1-regularization corresponds to subtracting the regression term

$$R(\boldsymbol{\beta}) = \lambda \sum_{i=0}^{m} |\beta_i| = \lambda \, \|\boldsymbol{\beta}\|_1 \,. \tag{4.17}$$

This is also known as LASSO-regularization and is originally used in the least squares setting. It has recently become a workhorse in machine learning because it tends to setting unimportant parameters to zero (sparsity) and thus resulting in a simpler and more interpretable model. This is especially true for problems with many features as shown in [46]. However we found that L_1-regularization did not give better results in our examples. In terms of a Bayesian point of view it can be seen as assuming a Laplacian distribution for the parameters $p(\boldsymbol{\beta}) = \frac{\lambda}{2}^N \exp(-\lambda \, \|\boldsymbol{\beta}\|_1)$. In Bayesian statistics the posterior distribution of the parameters $\boldsymbol{\beta}$ is proportional to the product of the likelihood $l(\boldsymbol{\beta})$ times the prior distribution $p(\boldsymbol{\beta})$ of $\boldsymbol{\beta}$. So the Bayesian point estimator for $\hat{\boldsymbol{\beta}}$ is

$$\hat{\boldsymbol{\beta}} = \max_{\boldsymbol{\beta}} l(\boldsymbol{\beta})p(\boldsymbol{\beta}). \tag{4.18}$$

Taking the logarithm of (4.18) and discarding the constant term results in

$$\hat{\boldsymbol{\beta}} = \max_{\boldsymbol{\beta}} L(\boldsymbol{\beta}) = \sum_{i=1}^{n}(y_i \ln \mu(\boldsymbol{x}_i, \boldsymbol{\beta}) + (1 - y_i)\ln(1 - \mu(\boldsymbol{x}_i, \boldsymbol{\beta})) - \lambda \, \|\boldsymbol{\beta}\|_1 \,. \tag{4.19}$$

Unfortunately, this function is not continuously differentiable so one cannot simply use standard gradient-based optimization methods. Nevertheless, this problem can be solved using a differentiable approximation of the regularization. An alternative setting of (4.19) in terms of a constraint optimization problem is given as

$$\min_{\boldsymbol{\beta}} - \sum_{i=1}^{n}(y_i \ln \mu(\boldsymbol{x}_i, \boldsymbol{\beta}) + (1 - y_i)\ln(1 - \mu(\boldsymbol{x}_i, \boldsymbol{\beta})), \tag{4.20}$$

$$\text{subject to } \|\boldsymbol{\beta}\|_1 \leq C.$$

Here the parameter $C > 0$ is related to the regularization parameter λ in a way that for every value λ there is a unique value C such that (4.19) and (4.20) have the same solution $\hat{\boldsymbol{\beta}}$.

4.4.2. L_2-**Regularization**

A more traditionally regularization is the L_2-regularization which is also known as ridge regression [30]. The regularized log-likelihood is

$$R(\beta) = \frac{\lambda}{2}\beta^\top\beta = \frac{\lambda}{2}\|\beta\|_2^2. \tag{4.21}$$

In optimization theory L_2-regularization is used to overcome singularity of the Hessian. Considering again the Bayesian point of view this corresponds to assuming a Gaussian distribution for the parameters $p(\beta) = \frac{1}{\sqrt{2\pi\sigma^2}}\exp\frac{\beta^\top\beta}{2\sigma^2}$ with zero mean and variance σ^2. Taking again the logarithm and discarding the constant term gives the L_2-regularized log-likelihood function

$$L(\beta) = \sum_{i=1}^{n}(y_i\ln\mu(\boldsymbol{x}_i,\beta) + (1-y_i)\ln(1-\mu(\boldsymbol{x}_i,\beta)) - \frac{\lambda}{2}\|\beta\|_2^2, \tag{4.22}$$

where $\lambda = \frac{1}{\sigma^2}$. This kind of regularization shrinks the parameter values towards zero. Hence a MLE $\hat{\beta}$ exists even with correlated features. Furthermore, the function given in (4.22) is twice continuously differentiable which enables the use of second-order optimization methods such as Newton-Raphson.

4.5. The TR-IRLS Algorithm

In this section, we state the truncated iteratively re-weighted least squares (TR-IRLS) algorithm proposed by Komarek [36]. We then analyze the lack of convergence that occurs sometimes and propose a slightly different formulation of the TR-IRLS algorithm in order to ensure convergence.

4.5.1. Solving the Maximum Likelihood Estimate Problem

After obtaining the formula for the deviance that is to be minimized it is still to be clarified how to solve

$$\min_{\beta} \operatorname{DEV}(\beta). \tag{4.23}$$

The standard approach is to apply the Newton-Raphson algorithm to the score equations. This is called iteratively re-weighted least squares (IRLS). The LR score equations are the first derivatives of the negative log-likelihood function with respect to the parameters β:

$$
\begin{aligned}
\frac{\partial}{\partial\beta_j}L(\beta) &= -\sum_{i=1}^{n}\left(y_i\frac{\frac{\partial}{\partial\beta_j}\mu(\boldsymbol{x}_i,\beta)}{\mu(\boldsymbol{x}_i,\beta)} - (1-y_i)\frac{\frac{\partial}{\partial\beta_j}\mu(\boldsymbol{x}_i,\beta)}{1-\mu(\boldsymbol{x}_i,\beta)}\right) \\
&= -\sum_{i=1}^{n}\left(y_i\frac{x_{ij}\mu(\boldsymbol{x}_i,\beta)(1-\mu(\boldsymbol{x}_i,\beta))}{\mu(\boldsymbol{x}_i,\beta)} - (1-y_i)\frac{x_{ij}\mu(\boldsymbol{x}_i,\beta)(1-\mu(\boldsymbol{x}_i,\beta))}{1-\mu(\boldsymbol{x}_i,\beta)}\right) \\
&= -\sum_{i=1}^{n}x_{ij}(y_i - \mu(\boldsymbol{x}_i,\beta)),
\end{aligned} \tag{4.24}
$$

where $j = 0,\ldots,m$ with m being the number of parameters. Differentiating with respect to all parameters gives the Jacobian $J(\beta)$. The score equations are equivalent to setting the Jacobian to zero, which results in a nonlinear system of equations.

Extending the definition of μ to $\mu(\boldsymbol{X},\beta) = (\mu(\boldsymbol{x}_1,\beta),\ldots,\mu(\boldsymbol{x}_n,\beta))^T$ enables us to write the score equations in matrix notation as

$$J(\beta) = -X^\top(y - \mu(X, \beta)) = 0. \tag{4.25}$$

Since the maximum likelihood function (4.6) is concave [48] there exist a unique global maximum which means the negative log-likelihood has a unique global minimum. The Newton-Raphson algorithm finds the solution of (4.25) through repeated linear approximations. After choosing an initial value β^0 a new guess for β^{k+1} is determined via the first-order approximation

$$\beta^{k+1} = \beta^k - H(\beta^k)^{-1}J(\beta^k), \tag{4.26}$$

where $H(\beta^k)$ describes the Hessian of the log-likelihood (4.7) evaluated at β^k. The Hessian is the matrix containing the second partial derivatives with respect to all parameters. The jl-th element of the Hessian is given by

$$\frac{\partial^2}{\partial\beta_j\partial\beta_l} = \sum_{i=1}^{n} x_{ij}x_{il}\mu(x_i, \beta)(1 - \mu(x_i, \beta)),$$

where $j, l = 0, \ldots, m$. To continue in matrix notation, we define a diagonal matrix $W \in \mathbb{R}^{n\times n}$ with the i-th diagonal element defined as $\mu(x_i, \beta)(1 - \mu(x_i, \beta))$. This enables us to write the Hessian as

$$H(\beta) = X^\top W X. \tag{4.27}$$

Using (4.27) and (4.25) the Newton-Raphson update formula (4.26) reads

$$\beta^{k+1} = \beta^k + (X^\top W X)^{-1}X^\top(y - \mu(X, \beta)). \tag{4.28}$$

Since $\beta^k = (X^\top W X)^{-1}X^\top W X\beta^k$ we may rewrite (4.28) as

$$\beta^{k+1} = (X^\top W X)^{-1}X^\top(W X\beta^k + (y - \mu(X, \beta)))$$
$$= (X^\top W X)^{-1}X^\top W z, \tag{4.29}$$

where $z = X\beta^k + W^{-1}(y - \mu(X, \beta))$. The elements of the vector z are called adjusted dependent covariates, since equation (4.29) may be seen as a weighted least squares problem with dependent variables z, see equation (3.11).

Solving this linear system of equations exactly, i.e. using a Cholesky factorization or calculating the inverse, is described in [36] with time complexity $\mathcal{O}(m^3 + mn)$. This is unacceptably slow for large dimensions. As a remedy, in [36], the authors have applied the idea of truncated Newton methods to solve (4.29). This method is called truncated IRLS (TR-IRLS). The idea is that the parameter β^k is only an approximation itself, hence there is no need to solve the linear system of equations (4.29) exactly. It is rather sufficient to get an approximate solution, e.g. by using the conjugate gradient method. The conjugate gradient method can then be terminated at early stages. Quoting from [36], we see that it is not exactly the same as a truncated Newton method.

> "The combination of IRLS and CG described earlier does not approximate the Newton direction. Instead, CG is applied to the weighted least squares regression that arises from the combination of the current position and the Newton direction. This linear system is different than that which describes the Newton direction alone, and we do not know whether the behavior of a truncated-Newton method would be identical to our IRLS and CG combination."

This means the Newton direction is implicitly calculated in the TR-IRLS approach and this needs to be taken into account when setting the termination condition for the CG algorithm. We did in fact observe divergence for some datasets, i.e. the norm of the gradient is not approaching zero. This problem is also reported in [38], where the authors tested TR-IRLS against their method using a trust region framework. To ensure convergence one has to consider the result from the theory of truncated Newton methods with CG. Following [20], we get convergence if the approximate solution $\boldsymbol{d}^k$ fulfills the upper bound

$$\left\|\nabla^2 L(\boldsymbol{\beta}^k)\boldsymbol{d}^k + \nabla L(\boldsymbol{\beta}^k)\right\|_2 \leq \eta_k \left\|\nabla L(\boldsymbol{\beta}^k)\right\|_2, \tag{4.30}$$

where $\eta_k < 1$. Since there might exist collinearity between covariates the Hessian is disturbed with a positive diagonal matrix in order to ensure positive definiteness. This stems from the L_2-regularization approach. There are two termination conditions for the conjugate gradient algorithm applied in [36]. One is the relative difference of two consecutive values of the deviance, i.e.,

$$\frac{\|\mathrm{DEV}_{k+1} - \mathrm{DEV}_k\|_2}{\|\mathrm{DEV}_{k+1}\|_2} < \epsilon_{\mathrm{DEV}} \tag{4.31}$$

The other uses the norm of the residuum in the k-th iteration

$$\boldsymbol{r}_k = (\boldsymbol{X}^\top \boldsymbol{W} \boldsymbol{X} + \lambda \boldsymbol{I})\boldsymbol{\beta}^k - \boldsymbol{X}^\top \boldsymbol{W} \boldsymbol{z}. \tag{4.32}$$

The algorithm is terminated if

$$\|\boldsymbol{r}_k\|_2 < \epsilon_r \|\boldsymbol{r}_0\|_2. \tag{4.33}$$

Since the Newton direction is calculated only implicitly in TR-IRLS, we need to unroll it which gives

$$\begin{aligned}
\|\boldsymbol{r}_{k+1}\|_2 =& \|(\boldsymbol{X}^\top \boldsymbol{W} \boldsymbol{X} + \lambda \boldsymbol{I})\boldsymbol{\beta}^{k+1} - \boldsymbol{X}^\top \boldsymbol{W} \boldsymbol{z}\|_2 \\
=& \|(\boldsymbol{X}^\top \boldsymbol{W} \boldsymbol{X} + \lambda \boldsymbol{I})\boldsymbol{\beta}^{k+1} - \boldsymbol{X}^\top \boldsymbol{W}(\boldsymbol{X}\boldsymbol{\beta}^k + \boldsymbol{W}^{-1}(\boldsymbol{y} - \mu(\boldsymbol{X}, \boldsymbol{\beta})))\|_2 \\
=& \|(\boldsymbol{X}^\top \boldsymbol{W} \boldsymbol{X} + \lambda \boldsymbol{I})(\boldsymbol{\beta}^k + \boldsymbol{d}^k) - (\boldsymbol{X}^\top \boldsymbol{W} \boldsymbol{X})\boldsymbol{\beta}^k - \boldsymbol{X}^\top(\boldsymbol{y} - \mu(\boldsymbol{X}, \boldsymbol{\beta}))\|_2 \\
=& \|\underbrace{(\boldsymbol{X}^\top \boldsymbol{W} \boldsymbol{X} + \lambda \boldsymbol{I})}_{\nabla^2 L(\boldsymbol{\beta}^k)} \boldsymbol{d}^k \underbrace{-\boldsymbol{X}^\top(\boldsymbol{y} - \mu(\boldsymbol{X}, \boldsymbol{\beta})) + \lambda \boldsymbol{\beta}^k}_{\nabla L(\boldsymbol{\beta}^k}\|_2
\end{aligned} \tag{4.34}$$

Comparing (4.34) and (4.30) we see the residual used for terminating the CG iterations is the same for TR-IRLS and classical truncated Newton. The parameter $\boldsymbol{\beta}^0$ is initialized with zero for all CG iterations in [36]. Therefore, we have $\boldsymbol{r}_0 = \boldsymbol{X}^\top \boldsymbol{W} \boldsymbol{z}$. Thus, for convergence of TR-IRLS we need

$$\epsilon_r \|\boldsymbol{X}^\top \boldsymbol{W} \boldsymbol{z}\|_2 \leq \eta_k \|\nabla L(\boldsymbol{\beta}^k)\|_2.$$

For the left-hand side we have

$$\begin{aligned}
\epsilon_r \|\boldsymbol{X}^\top \boldsymbol{W} \boldsymbol{z}\|_2 =& \epsilon_r \|(\boldsymbol{X}^\top \boldsymbol{W} \boldsymbol{X})\boldsymbol{\beta}^k + \boldsymbol{X}^\top(\boldsymbol{y} - \mu(\boldsymbol{X}, \boldsymbol{\beta}))\|_2 \\
=& \epsilon_r \|\underbrace{(\boldsymbol{X}^\top \boldsymbol{W} \boldsymbol{X})\boldsymbol{\beta}^k + \lambda \boldsymbol{\beta}^k}_{\nabla^2 L(\boldsymbol{\beta}_k)} \underbrace{-\lambda \boldsymbol{\beta}^k + \boldsymbol{X}^\top(\boldsymbol{y} - \mu(\boldsymbol{X}, \boldsymbol{\beta}))}_{-\nabla L(\boldsymbol{\beta}^k)}\|_2.
\end{aligned} \tag{4.35}$$

While in (4.35) the term for $\nabla L(\boldsymbol{\beta}^k)$ goes to zero as the CG iteration increases, this is not the case for the Hessian of the likelihood function. Hence the norm will not approach zero and a convergence of the TR-IRLS algorithm is not guaranteed. As a remedy for this we simply take the right-hand side of (4.30) as termination criterion which results in the classic truncated Newton approach. Figure 4.3 shows the evolution of the gradient of the regularized likelihood

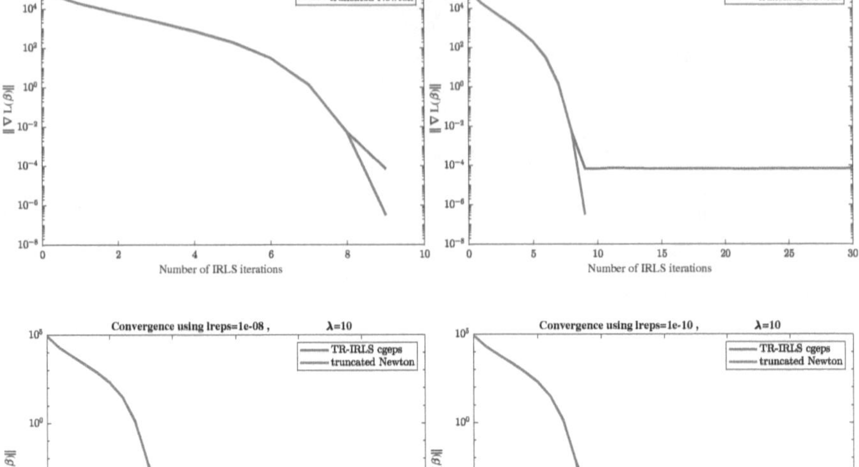

Fig. 4.3.: Convergence results for dataset ds1.100 with $\epsilon_r = 10^{-4}$(TR-IRLS), $\eta_k = 10^{-4}$(truncated Newton).

function for the TR-IRLS algorithm with termination condition (4.33) and our suggestion to use (4.30) instead.

Another solution to the problem would be to assign a much smaller value to ϵ_r to compensate for $\|r_0\|$ not approaching zero. This will give convergence but, first of all, it is not clear how small to choose the value for different datasets and, secondly, for the first IRLS iterations the system of equations would be solved with a very good precision resulting in a lot of unnecessary CG iterations. This fact is demonstrated in Figure 4.4. Therefore, from now on we use the TR-IRLS algorithm with the classic truncated Newton termination criteria given in (4.30).

4.5.2. Singular Value Decomposition

In the case of only a few covariates but many datapoints, as it is the case for geological applications, it is possible to calculate the Hessian explicitly because it has a small dimension. This is computationally expensive but will also give very accurate solutions for β_k. This leads to the idea of using singular value decomposition (SVD) to obtain a solution of the equation (4.29). The SVD of the Hessian is

$$\nabla^2 L(\beta) = U\Sigma V^\top, \tag{4.36}$$

where the unitary matrices $U \in \mathbb{R}^{m \times m}, V \in \mathbb{R}^{m \times m}$ and the diagonal matrix $\Sigma \in \mathbb{R}^{m \times m}$ that contains all singular values $\sigma_i, i = 1, \ldots, m$ of the Hessian $\nabla^2 L(\beta)$ with $\sigma_1 > \sigma_2 > \cdots >$

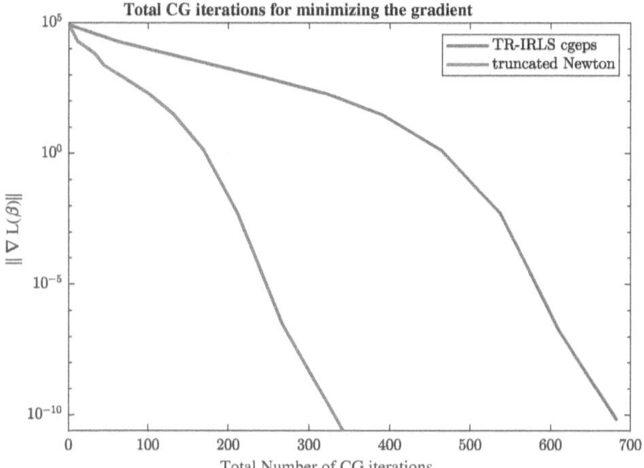

Fig. 4.4.: Setting $\epsilon_r = 10^{-10}$ in the TR-IRLS algorithm results in convergence for the ds1.100 dataset. But the number of total CG iterations is approximately twice as large as the number with truncated Newton termination.

$\sigma_m > 0$ [43]. This decomposition can now be used to get a new iterate of IRLS by substituting the Hessian in equation (4.29) by (4.36), which leads to

$$\beta^{k+1} = V\Sigma^{-1}U^\top X^\top W z, \tag{4.37}$$

where Σ^{-1} is obtained by just inverting the diagonal elements of Σ. Note that we never compute actual matrix products but rather perform multiple multiplications of a matrix with a vector

$$\beta^{k+1} = V(\Sigma^{-1}(U^\top(X^\top(W z)))). \tag{4.38}$$

We implemented the use of the SVD as a backup for cases in which the conjugate gradient algorithm failed to reduce the deviance.

4.6. Rare Events

When dealing with rare events data there are some issues one needs to consider. Rare events occur with a significantly smaller frequency than common events. So classifying rare events correctly has usually a greater value. The rare class presents some problems to existing classification algorithms such as logistic regression. King and Zeng [33] state that the problems in logistic regression caused by rare events stem from two sources. Statistical methods such as logistic regression underestimate the probability of rare events and tend to be biased towards the majority class which is the less important class. A second problem is that common data collection strategies are inefficient for rare events. As a remedy, King and Zeng propose endogenous sampling with some corrections.

4.6.1. Sample Selection Bias

Following Zadrozny [65], let s be a binary value that is one when a sample is selected and zero otherwise. Zadrozny listed four cases regarding the dependence of s on the sample (x, y)

- s is independent of x and y, then there is no bias at all,

- s is independent of y given x ($P(s|x,y) = P(s|x)$), then there is a feature bias,

- s is independent of x given y ($P(s|x,y) = P(s|y)$), then there is a class bias which corresponds to changing the prior probability of the class y,

- s is dependent on both x and y, then there is a full bias.

In [65], the author states that the LR model is not affected by sample selection bias, which is the second case above. However, when sampling is dependent on the response variable the LR model is affected by the class bias. This corresponds to the third case above.
So with choice-based sampling in rare events the standard likelihood function is inconsistent. To see this, consider the joint distribution of X and y in the sample

$$f_s(X, y|\beta) = P_s(X|y, \beta)P_s(y). \tag{4.39}$$

Since the sampling was independent of X the conditional probability of x is the same in the population and in the sample, i.e.

$$P_s(X|y, \beta) = P(X|y, \beta). \tag{4.40}$$

However, the conditional probability of X in the population can be described as

$$P(X|y, \beta) = \frac{f(y, X|\beta)}{P(y)} \tag{4.41}$$

and the joint probability of X and y in the population is

$$P(X, y|\beta) = P(y|X, \beta)P(X) \tag{4.42}$$

and hence substituting and rearranging yields

$$f_s(X, y|\beta) = \frac{P_s(y)}{P(y)}P(y|X, \beta)P(X) \tag{4.43}$$

$$= \frac{H}{Q}P(y|X, \beta)P(X), \tag{4.44}$$

where $\frac{H}{Q} = \frac{P_s(y)}{P(y)}$, with H and Q representing the proportions in the sample and in the population, respectively. The likelihood function is then

$$l_{\text{endogenous}} = \prod_{i=1}^{n} \frac{H_i}{Q_i}P(y_i|x_i, \beta)P(x_i). \tag{4.45}$$

Therefore, when dealing with REs and imbalanced data using choice-based sampling, the likelihood (4.45) is the one that needs to be maximized.

4.6.2. Logistic Regression with Endogenous Sampling

King and Zeng stated two possible solutions to correct the sample bias which both go back to Manski and Lerman [40].

Prior Correction

Prior correction involves the maximization of the usual logistic regression likelihood (4.6) and then correcting the estimates based on prior information about the population. Let τ and $\bar{y}$ be the fraction of ones in the population and in the sample, respectively. With choice-based sampling the MLE $\hat{\beta}$ is statistically inconsistent. However, as stated in [33], this inconsistency is only due to the estimate of the bias $\hat{\beta}_0$ while the $\hat{\beta}_1, \ldots, \hat{\beta}_m$ are statistically consistent estimates of $\beta_1, \ldots, \beta_m$. In order to obtain a consistent estimate $\tilde{\beta}_0$ for β_0 one has to correct the obtained $\hat{\beta}_0$ from the MLE as follows:

$$\tilde{\beta}_0 = \hat{\beta}_0 - \ln\left[\left(\frac{1-\tau}{\tau}\right)\left(\frac{\bar{y}}{1-\bar{y}}\right)\right]. \tag{4.46}$$

Prior correction is easy to use. However, if the model is misspecified, estimates of β are less robust than weighting, a method that is introduced next.

Weighting

Manski and Lerman introduced the Weighted Exogenous Sampling Maximum Likelihood (WESML). They proved that the estimator is consistent and asymptotically normal as long as knowledge of the population probability is available. So the log-likelihood for LR can be rewritten as

$$
\begin{aligned}
L(\beta|\boldsymbol{y}, \boldsymbol{X}) &= -\sum_{i=1}^{n} \ln P(y_i|\boldsymbol{x}_i, \beta) \\
&= -\sum_{i=1}^{n} \frac{Q_i}{H_i} \ln P(y_i|\boldsymbol{x}_i, \beta) \\
&= -\sum_{i=1}^{n} w_i(y_i \ln \mu(\boldsymbol{x}_i, \beta) + (1-y_i)\ln(1-\mu(\boldsymbol{x}_i, \beta)), \tag{4.47}
\end{aligned}
$$

where $w_i = \frac{Q_i}{H_i} = (\frac{\tau}{\bar{y}})y_i + (\frac{1-\tau}{1-\bar{y}})(1-y_i)$. Weighting is asymptotically less consistent than prior correction. This can be seen in small samples, although the difference is not large. However, when both a large sample is available and the model is misspecified then weighting can outperform prior correction. According to [33], weighting is preferable to prior correction.

4.6.3. Weighted Logistic Regression

Referring to the results and recommendations of the authors in [33], we use weighting to correct the sample bias. The log-likelihood function to consider is given in (4.47). The corresponding Jacobian is given as

$$\boldsymbol{J}(\beta) = -\boldsymbol{X}^\top \boldsymbol{D}(\boldsymbol{y} - \mu(\boldsymbol{X}, \beta)), \tag{4.48}$$

where $\boldsymbol{D} \in \mathbb{R}^{n \times n}$ denotes a diagonal matrix with diagonal entries $d_{ii} = w_i$. The Hessian is given as

$$\boldsymbol{H}(\beta) = \boldsymbol{X}^\top \widetilde{\boldsymbol{W}} \boldsymbol{X} \tag{4.49}$$

with $\widetilde{\boldsymbol{W}} = \boldsymbol{W}\boldsymbol{D}$. This results in the Newton-Raphson update

$$
\begin{aligned}
\beta^{k+1} &= (\boldsymbol{X}^\top \widetilde{\boldsymbol{W}} \boldsymbol{X})^{-1} \boldsymbol{X}^\top \widetilde{\boldsymbol{W}}(\boldsymbol{X}\beta^k + \boldsymbol{W}^{-1}(\boldsymbol{y} - \mu(\boldsymbol{X}, \beta))) \\
&= (\boldsymbol{X}^\top \widetilde{\boldsymbol{W}} \boldsymbol{X})^{-1} \boldsymbol{X}^\top \widetilde{\boldsymbol{W}} \boldsymbol{z}, \tag{4.50}
\end{aligned}
$$

with $\boldsymbol{z}$ being the same as in equation (4.29).

4.7. Model Selection Strategies

Model selection comes into play whenever there are more than just a few covariates. It should always be the goal of a model selection method to choose the "best" model. Thereby, the "best" model depends on the scientific context but most commonly it means to obtain a model that uses as few covariates as possible while still explaining the outcome to a desired degree. There are basically three types of selection strategies:

- Best subset selection

- Stepwise selection

- Purposeful selection

The **best subset selection** calculates the log-likelihood value for all models containing the intercept and p predictors with $p = 0, \ldots, m$ where m is the total number of predictors available. It then chooses the best model with p covariates for every p by choosing the one with the largest log-likelihood value. From this $m + 1$ models the overall "best" is chosen depending on the criterion chosen for "best". There are several criteria available. In [32] it is recommended to choose Mallows C_p or the Akaike Information Criterion (AIC).

The **stepwise selection** covers two different approaches, namely forward and backward selection. Forward selection starts with the null model M_0, i.e. the model consisting only of the intercept. Its log-likelihood is denoted by L_0. Next, each of the possible m models consisting of the intercept and one covariate is fitted. Their corresponding log-likelihood values are calculated and the likelihood ratio test for each model versus the null model M_0 is performed. The model resulting in the smallest p-value is denoted as model M_1 and the corresponding predictor is considered the "most-important" variable. However there is a threshold p_E ("E" for entry) for a variable to be included into the model. The p-value should fall below that threshold in order for the covariate to be included in the model. A value for p_E in the range of 0.15 to 0.20 is suggested in [32]. If no predictor fulfills this condition the model selection stops. This procedure is then continued for the remaining $m - 1$ covariates resulting in models $M_2, \ldots, M_k$ with $k \leq m$ denoting the number of variables that exhibit a p-value smaller than the threshold for the likelihood ratio test. The "best" model out of $M_0, \ldots, M_k$ is again chosen using a criteria such as AIC or C_p. Backward selection starts with a full model, i.e. M_m. One predictor is then removed and the log-likelihood value is calculated by fitting the model. This is done for all m covariates and the model resulting in the smallest p-value in the likelihood ratio test chosen as model M_{m-1}. Again there is a threshold p_R ("R" for remove) that should be exceeded by the p-value of the likelihood ratio test in order for a covariate to be removed. The suggested range of p_R is also 0.15 to 0.20. Additionally, a combination of both stepwise selections is possible. Thus after a forward selection step the removal of one of the current variables in the model is tested.

Purposeful selection is suggested in [32] and involves seven steps that are time consuming and need a lot of interaction with a human being. These steps are only summarized briefly.

(*Step 1*): A careful univariable analysis is performed to identify possible candidates for a first multivariable model. The researcher should consider the Wald statistic as well as the likelihood ratio test as criteria to identify the significance of the variable. A significance level for the p-value as large as 0.20 to 0.25 is suggested since studies [10, 29] have shown that a more traditional level of 0.05 often fails to identify variables that are known to be important.

(*Step 2*): Fit the model with all significant variables from step 1. Assess the importance of each covariate using the Wald statistic. Eliminate variables with p-values greater than the threshold (i.e. $\alpha = 0.05$) and compare the smaller models to the old model using the likelihood ratio test.

(*Step 3*): From the fit of the smaller model compare the values of the estimated coefficients from that smaller model to their values in the larger model. If the values changed noticeably one should review the eliminated variables and add them back one at a time because one or more variables might have been important for variables that remained in the model. This should be performed slowly by repeating step 2 and step 3 until all important variables appear to be in the model

(*Step 4*): Each variable not selected in step 1 is added to the model obtained at the end of step 3, once at a time. Their significance is checked using the Wald statistic or the likelihood ratio test. This ensures that variables that are unimportant by themselves but contribute in the presence of other variables are included in the model.

(*Step 5*): Check for each variable that the logit increases/decreases linearly as a function of the covariate. The resulting model is referred to as *main effects model*.

(*Step 6*): Check for interactions among the variables in the main effects model. The inclusion of an interaction term should be based on statistical as well as practical considerations.

(*Step 7*): Before applying the final model one needs to check its fit.

This type of model building is undoubtedly the one that should be applied if possible. However, it takes a lot of time and work from a researcher that in the best case is an expert in the field from where the dataset is from. Thus in practice, forward and backward selection which is provided in many statistical packages is used.

4.8. Artificial Neural Networks

An artificial neural network (ANN) is inspired by the design of the human brain which is built of very complex webs of interconnected neurons. However, to state it in a simpler manner: ANNs are just compositions of nonlinear functions applied to linear combinations of variables. ANNs are widely used in practice and there exist several different types of neural networks depending on the application they are intended for. A detailed description can be found in [11, 27]. The multilayer-perceptron is the one considered here. The general form consists of an input layer, a number of hidden layers and one output layer. In every layer there are a number of neurons which are all linked to every neuron in the next layer. The input layer consists of the covariates and the bias. The number of neurons in the hidden layers is a user decision. The output layer usually only has one neuron in classification problems. This output neuron has a value ranging between zero and one. This potential describes the confidence of the network for the given data. If the network consists of more than one hidden layer, one speaks of deep learning. The general output of a K-layer ANN is given as

$$\sigma(\boldsymbol{W}, \boldsymbol{b}, \boldsymbol{x}_i) = \Lambda_K \left(\boldsymbol{b}^{(K)} + \boldsymbol{W}^{(K)} \Lambda_{K-1} \left(\boldsymbol{b}^{(K-1)} + \boldsymbol{W}^{(K-1)} \cdots \Lambda_1 \left(\boldsymbol{b}^{(1)} + \boldsymbol{W}^{(1)} \boldsymbol{x}_i \right) \right) \right). \tag{4.51}$$

The $\Lambda_k, k = 1, \ldots, K$, describe nonlinear activation functions, which, of course, can also all be the same. The $\boldsymbol{b}^{(k)} \in \mathbb{R}^{J_k}$ are vectors containing the bias values. The $\boldsymbol{W}^{(k)} \in \mathbb{R}^{J_k \times J_{k-1}}$ are matrices containing the weights from layer $(k-1)$ with J_{k-1} neurons to layer k with J_k neurons. Here we have $J_0 = m$ being the number of predictors. By $\boldsymbol{w}$ we denote the vector containing all weights. It consists of M elements where M can become very large. Figure 4.5 shows a neural network with two hidden layers and four neurons in each hidden layer. The training of a neural network aims to find the optimal weights $\boldsymbol{w}^* = (\boldsymbol{w}_1^*, \ldots, \boldsymbol{w}_M^*)^T$. To find these weights the minimization of an error function is performed. Usually, this is the squared error

$$E(\boldsymbol{w}) = \sum_{i=1}^{n} (y_i - \sigma(\boldsymbol{\beta}, \boldsymbol{x}_i))^2. \tag{4.52}$$

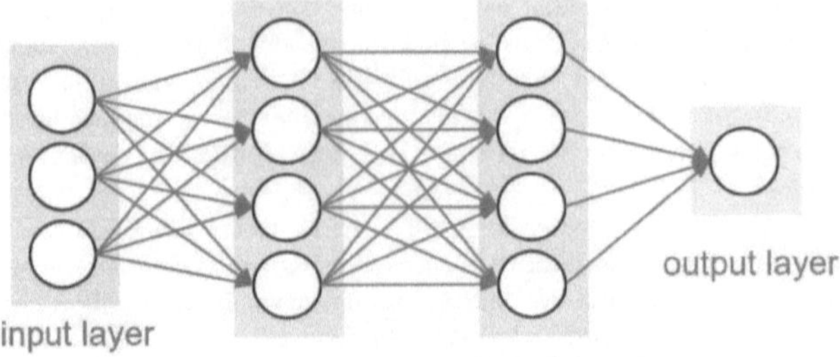

Fig. 4.5.: Example of an neural network with two hidden layers and four neurons in each layer. Picture taken from [56].

In classification problems the error function should be the cross-entropy

$$E(\boldsymbol{w}) = \sum_{i=1}^{n} (y_i \log(\sigma(\boldsymbol{w}, \boldsymbol{x}_i)) + (1 - y_i \log(1 - \sigma(\boldsymbol{w}, \boldsymbol{x}_i)). \tag{4.53}$$

For either error function this is a nonlinear optimization problem. Different methods have been proposed for training a neural network. They are all based on the update formula

$$\boldsymbol{w}^{k+1} = \boldsymbol{w}^k + \eta_k \boldsymbol{d}_k, \tag{4.54}$$

where k is the current iteration, $\boldsymbol{w}^0 \in \mathbb{R}^M$ is a given initial weight, η_k is the learning rate which corresponds to the step length in optimization theory and $\boldsymbol{d}_k \in \mathbb{R}^M$ is the search direction. Most of the times the search direction is the negative gradient, i.e. $\boldsymbol{d}_k = -\nabla E(\boldsymbol{w})$. In order to determine the direction $\boldsymbol{d}_k$, the derivative of the error function with respect to every weight is required. Straight forward computation of the derivatives would require $\mathcal{O}(M^2)$ operations, which is too expansive.

4.8.1. Backpropagation

Backpropagation was first introduced by Rumelhardt et. al. in 1986 [49]. The basic idea is to use the chain rule twice to evaluate the error backwards through the network to get the derivative of the error function with respect to every weight $\nabla E(\boldsymbol{w})$. This techniques reduces the computational cost from $\mathcal{O}(M^2)$ to $\mathcal{O}(M)$. Therefore, basically every minimization algorithm used for minimizing the error function that uses first order information makes use of backpropagation. Often the gradient is not calculated over the whole set of training samples but only calculated on batches. A batch is a subset of the training data. This speeds up calculations.

4.8.2. Neural Networks in the Context of Logistic Regression

In this section, we describe the deployment of a multi-layer perceptron (MLP) starting with a simple logistic regression model. Thus consider the prediction for y on some data $\boldsymbol{x}$ through the logistic function

$$\mu(\boldsymbol{x}, \boldsymbol{\beta}) \approx y.$$

This results in the logit function

$$g(\mu) = \beta_0 + \boldsymbol{\beta}^T \boldsymbol{x},$$

where this time there is no intercept term $x_0 \equiv 1$ in $\boldsymbol{x}$. Assume now that the prediction μ is not good enough, and we want to improve it. This can be done by adding more terms to the logit, and thus adding more degrees of freedom. This can be formalized by

$$g(\mu) = \beta_0 + \boldsymbol{\beta}^T \boldsymbol{x} + \sum_{k=1}^{K} \beta_{l_k} F_k(\boldsymbol{x}) = \beta_0 + \sum_{k=1}^{K} \beta_k F_k(\boldsymbol{x}),$$

where $F_k : \mathbb{R}^m \rightarrow \mathbb{R}$ are functions. In the second representation we simply add the inner product of $\boldsymbol{\beta}$ and $\boldsymbol{x}$ to the sum. For simplicity consider $\boldsymbol{x} = (x_1, x_2)$. The explanation can also be generalize to more predictor variables. Let us define five functions $F_1(x), \ldots, F_5(x)$ with

- $F_1(x) = x_1$

- $F_2(x) = x_2$

- $F_3(x) = x_1^2$

- $F_4(x) = x_2^2$

- $F_5(x) = x_1 x_2$

Setting $F = (F_1, \ldots F_5)$ this would lead the the new logit

$$g(\mu) = \beta_0 + \beta_1 x_1 + \beta_2 x_2 + \beta_3 x_1^2 + \beta_4 x_2^2 + \beta_5 x_1 x_2 = \beta_0 + \tilde{\boldsymbol{\beta}}^T F(\boldsymbol{x}),$$

where $\tilde{\boldsymbol{\beta}} = (\beta_1, \ldots, \beta_5)^T$. With this definitions we moved from a logit that is linear in $\boldsymbol{x}$ to a logit that is quadratic in $\boldsymbol{x}$ (but linear in $F(\boldsymbol{x})$). This adds three more degrees of freedom and thus the model is able to better fit the data $\boldsymbol{x}$ to the outcome y.

How do we know that a quadratic logit is adequate to fit the data? Well, we do not know! The idea is now to learn the best functions $F_k(x)$ directly from the data. Instead of explicitly defining the functions F_k, we use a general non-linear function Λ applied to the linear combination of our data $\boldsymbol{x}$. The parameters of the linear combination are called *weights*. Let us now leave the example with two predictor variables and return to the general case of m predictor variables. For a predefined number K we have the K functions $\Lambda(b_1 + \boldsymbol{w}_1^T \boldsymbol{x}), \ldots, \Lambda(b_K + \boldsymbol{w}_K^T \boldsymbol{x})$, where $\boldsymbol{w}_i = (w_{i1}, \ldots, w_{im})^T$. Extending this to matrix notation and inserting it into the logit gives

$$g(\mu) = \beta_0 + \tilde{\boldsymbol{\beta}}^T \Lambda(\boldsymbol{b} + \boldsymbol{W} \boldsymbol{x})$$

Applying now the logistic function to the logit to get the predicted output gives

$$\mu(\boldsymbol{x}, \beta_0, \tilde{\boldsymbol{\beta}}, \boldsymbol{b}, \boldsymbol{W}) = \mu \left(\beta_0 + \tilde{\boldsymbol{\beta}}^T \Lambda(\boldsymbol{b} + \boldsymbol{W} \boldsymbol{x}) \right)$$

If we now simply rename

$$\beta_0 \rightarrow \boldsymbol{b}^{(2)},$$
$$\tilde{\boldsymbol{\beta}} \rightarrow \boldsymbol{W}^{(2)},$$
$$\boldsymbol{b} \rightarrow \boldsymbol{b}^{(1)},$$
$$\boldsymbol{W} \rightarrow \boldsymbol{W}^{(1)},$$
$$\Lambda \rightarrow \Lambda_1,$$
$$\mu \rightarrow \Lambda_2,$$

and compare it to (4.51); we see that we derived the output of a MLP with one hidden layer.

The above way of deriving neural networks is intended to show the evolution from logistic regression to neural networks. It shows the much greater ability of neural networks to fit arbitrary functions. However, when we performed the step of replacing the explicit parametric function definitions F_k by a non-linear function of the scalar product, we sacrificed a lot of insight. We want to maintain the explicit function representation and try to find the best such representation in a given model space. The next chapter will explain this in detail.

Part III.

Proposed Logistic Regression Method

5. Logistic Regression Classification

5.1. Preliminaries

Neural networks are often able to deliver far better predictions than standard logistic regression as they can be considered a generalization; see section 4.8.2. The downside of ANN approaches is that, typically, little insight can be gained from the trained network, making it hard to gain a better understanding of the setting of the problem. This is mainly the result of their black box character. The advantage of maintaining an explicit model would be to have explicit causality and a lot of statistical characteristics from which the user can derive knowledge about the underlying problem. The selection of appropriate non-linearities in the logit is supposed to work in an automatic manner without the need of interaction with a researcher. However, this is only intended to guide the researcher in the process of finding the best model. The general idea is explained in the next sections.

5.1.1. Transforming the Input Space

The idea to transform the input data into a higher dimensional space is not new. Cover's theorem states that every complex pattern is more likely to be linearly separable if it is cast in a higher dimensional space by a non-linear transformation [17]. The intuition behind this is the following. Lifting n points onto the vertices of the simplex in $n-1$ dimension using a non-linear transformation makes ever partition of the samples into two sets linearly separable. An example is the two dimensional set of datapoints that are arranged in a circle. The positive targets are located inside a circle with radius r. The negative targets are located outside the circle (see Figure 5.1).

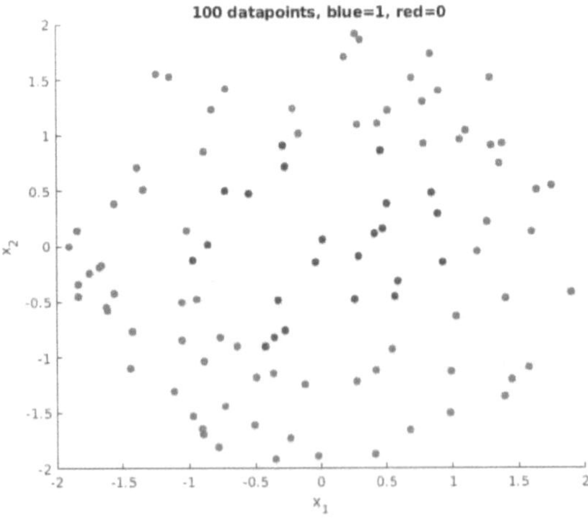

Fig. 5.1.: Example data which is generated such that all points within radius 1 of the origin are positive.

This dataset is clearly not linearly separable. Lifting the data to a higher dimensional space with a non-linear transformation will result in a linearly separable dataset. See Figure 5.2, where the data was lifted into a three dimensional space. The transformation here could be to assign a larger x_3-value to a point the further away this point is from the middle of the circle.

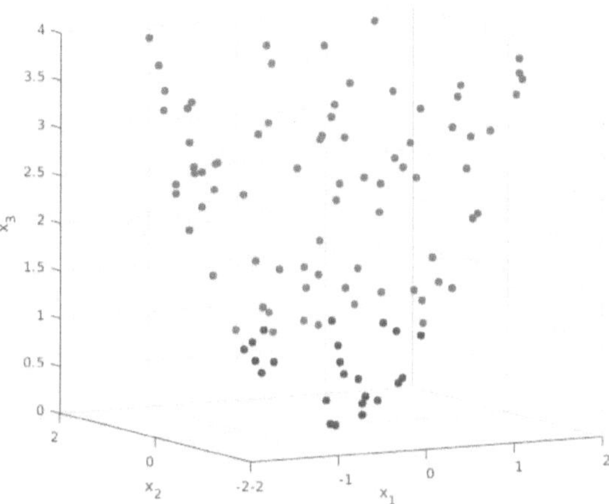

Fig. 5.2.: Same dataset as in figure 5.1, but now in 3D with an additional degree of freedom.

Now, we train two neural networks on this dataset and see how they perform. For the first one, we choose the number of hidden neurons to be three. The second one has four hidden neurons. The maximum number of epochs was 10.000 and the threshold for the gradient was $1 \cdot 10^{-6}$, i.e. the training is stopped if the norm of the gradient reaches a value below that threshold.

Due to the random initialization of the neural network the results vary. With three units in the hidden layer really no run was able to represent the underlying truth. With four units in the hidden layer there are satisfying results. But there are also runs which converged to a local minimum, resulting in a bad prediction.

A larger number of hidden units predicts the test set more reliably for almost every run. However, with too many hidden units the network can overfit on the training data which, in turn, will decrease the accuracy of the predictions on unseen data. This is illustrated in Figure 5.5. These are still the same datapoints, but now we changed the value of some of the points from negative to positive i.e., we have introduced some noise. The test set did not change. As one can see, the neural network overfits the training data in terms of trying to correctly predict every positive point. The ideal number of hidden neurons can only be chosen heuristically and is different for every dataset.

Let us now run a logistic regression model. Not only with x_1 and x_2 as variables but also including the squares of both coordinates. This is a logistic regression model with four predictors, i.e.

$$\mu(\boldsymbol{x}, \boldsymbol{\beta}) = \frac{\exp(\beta_0 + \beta_1 x_1 + \beta_2 x_2 + \beta_3 x_1^2 + \beta_4 x_2^2)}{1 + \exp(\beta_0 + \beta_1 x_1 + \beta_2 x_2 + \beta_3 x_1^2 + \beta_4 x_2^2)}.$$

This model will yield the same result for every run since there is no random initialization necessary. We used a regularization term ($\lambda = 0.1$) to prevent the parameters from becoming

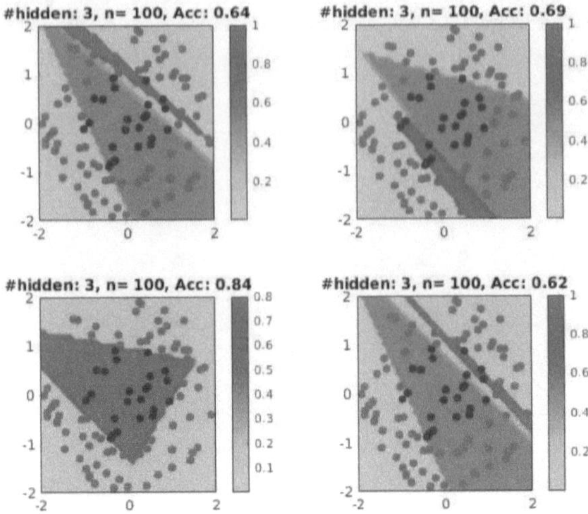

Fig. 5.3.: Neural network with three hidden neurons. The accuracy was measured with an independent test set that was generated the same way as the training data.

too large. This might happen because it does not matter how large the parameters are for x_1^2 and x_2^2 as long as they have the same value. Figure 5.6 shows the resulting prediction of the LR model. We also state the accuracy (see section 5.4) on the test data. Our logistic regression approach outperforms the one of the neural network with seven hidden neurons. It is also worth mentioning that we have no sharp decision boundary where on the one side everything is assigned 1 and on the other side everything is assigned 0. Instead there is an area of conditional probability between 0.4 and 0.6 which expresses the uncertainty of the prediction.

The decision boundary of the solution in the four dimensional space (x_1, x_2, x_1^2, x_2^2) is a hyperplane that separates the data. Transforming it back to the two dimensional space (x_1, x_2) this is a non-linear boundary. In this example this can be calculated explicitly. The decision boundary where the predicted conditional probability is 0.5 can be calculated by setting the logit to zero, i.e. $g(\mu) = \boldsymbol{\beta}^\top \boldsymbol{x} = 0$. This is the case because

$$\mu(\boldsymbol{x}, \boldsymbol{\beta}) = \frac{\exp(g)}{1 + \exp(g)} = \frac{\exp(0)}{1 + \exp(0)} = \frac{1}{2}$$

This yields

$$\beta_0 + \beta_1 x_1 + \beta_2 x_2 + \beta_3 x_1^2 + \beta_4 x_2^2 = 0,$$

which can be transformed to the equation of an ellipse $\frac{(x_1 - Mx_1)^2}{a} + \frac{(x_2 - Mx_2)^2}{b} = 1$ with a, b being the radius of the horizontal and vertical axis, respectively. Mx_1 and Mx_2 denote the midpoint of the ellipse. Performing this transformation results in

$$Mx_1 = \frac{\beta_1}{2\beta_3}, \quad Mx_2 = \frac{\beta_2}{2\beta_4}, \quad a = \sqrt{\frac{\beta_1 + \beta_2 - 2\beta_0}{2\beta_3}}, \quad b = \sqrt{\frac{\beta_1 + \beta_2 - 2\beta_0}{2\beta_4}}.$$

For the datapoints given, we have

$$Mx_1 = -0.030, \quad Mx_2 = -0.021, \quad Mx_1 = 1.015, \quad Mx_2 = 0.960,$$

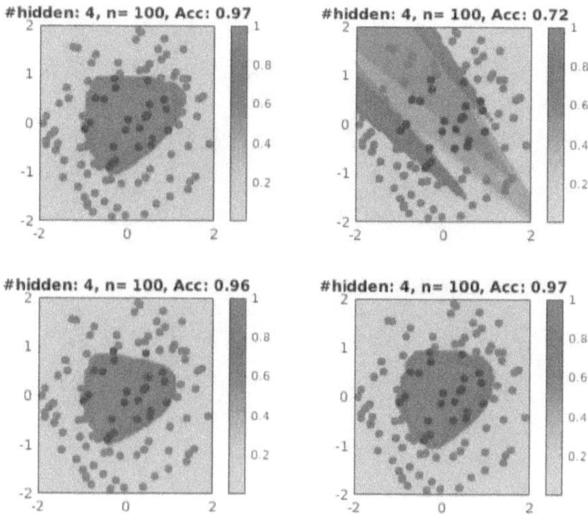

Fig. 5.4.: Neural network with four hidden neurons. The accuracy was measured with an independent test set that was generated the same way as the training data.

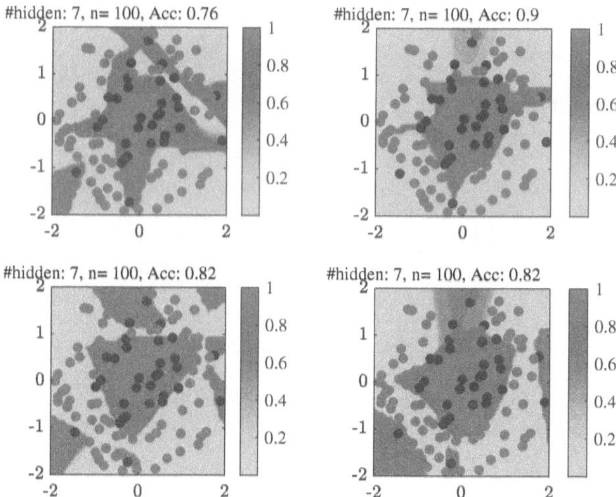

Fig. 5.5.: Neural network with seven hidden neurons. The training data now contains some outliers. The neural network tries to predict the outliers correctly which leads to a decrease in accuracy on the test set.

which is basically the ground truth that was used to generate the data, as shown in Figure 5.6.

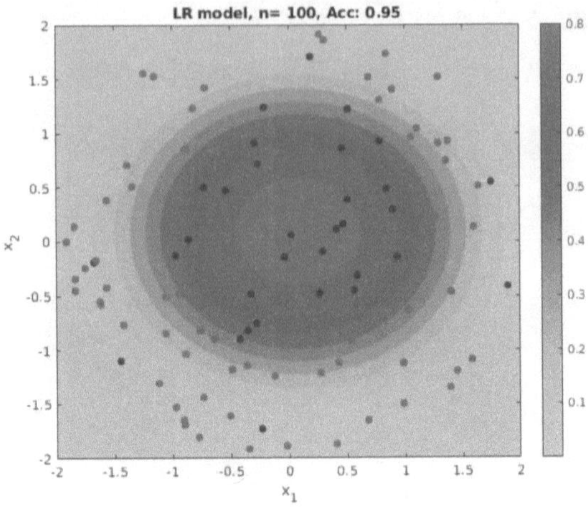

Fig. 5.6.: Logistic regression model with additional terms x_1^2, x_2^2. The training data now contains some outliers. The model is not affected by the outliers and gives better prediction accuracy as the neural network with seven hidden units.

5.2. Selection of Non-linearities

The example above shows that logistic regression can be a powerful method for classification. However, the example was designed such that it was easy to find the non-linearities which improve the model and predictions. In a real world setting the underlying truth is barely explainable with such a simple model. Several problems can occur. Firstly, even if the ground truth follows a possibly simple representation of some variables it is not guaranteed that all of the significant variables can be collected. Thus, some variables that would be needed for a perfect representation might simply not be available. Secondly, even if all critical variables are available the ground truth might consist of very complicated non-linearities (exponential of variables, discontinuous dependencies, etc.).

The two challenges to tackle are, on the one hand, the definition of non-linearities that are taken into consideration and, on the other hand, the selection of the important non-linearities out of the whole set of considered non-linearities. Since the main goal is to obtain an interpretable model it is natural to assume an underlying ground truth that is not too complex. As a starting point, we include only squares and two-fold interactions of covariates. This enables the model to finding an quadratic decision boundary in the original space $\in \mathbb{R}^m$ of the covariables. The indices of the candidates are stored in the set $\mathcal{I}$. For three covariables x_1, x_2, x_3 the set $\mathcal{I}$ would be

$$\mathcal{I} = \big\{\{1\}, \{2\}, \{3\}, \{1,1\}, \{2,2\}, \{3,3\}, \{1,2\}, \{1,3\}, \{2,3\}\big\}.$$

Denoting by $\tilde{m}$ the number of elements in the set $\mathcal{I}$, i.e. the covariates plus the non-linearities, there are $2^{\tilde{m}}$ possible models that can be created out of $\tilde{m}$ variables. A dataset with 20 covariables results in $\tilde{m} = 20 + 20 + \binom{20}{2} = 230$, which in turn results in $2^{230} = 1.7 \cdot 10^{69}$ possible models. Thus it is clear that a brute force trial-and-error of all models is infeasible. This is where we enter the field of model selection. Since the suggested procedure is mainly conceived for prospectivity modeling we can take advantage of two properties of the respective datasets. Firstly, a large amount of data is available since the area of investigation is usually large and a lot of samples are taken in order to cover that area. Furthermore, the number of samples increases in case of a three dimensional model since there is an additional dimension for every predictor. Secondly, there are not too many covariates involved, making it feasible to choose the approach with hand crafted non-linearities.

The model selection process is performed in two main steps. In the first step, the majority of unimportant non-linearities is discarded. In the second step a more careful selection of non-linearities and covariates is performed.

The method uses standard statistical methods. These are combined and adapted to perform well on rare event data. The development of the method is inspired by two fabricated datasets. To show that the method works on real world data, we compare it to neural networks and a model selection function implemented in MATLAB. The datasets are introduced in 5.3.

5.3. Datasets

We generate two fabricated datasets where the ground truth and the maximum likelihood estimation of the true parameters are known beforehand. Furthermore, we use real datasets that come from different fields. These are described in the next subsection. Of course it would be advantageous to have as many datasets as possible from the field of prospectivity modeling. These datasets are not easy to get. However, we have access to a dataset provided by Beak Consultants GmbH based in Freiberg, Saxony, Germany. Beak is a service company in the geoscience, environmental and IT sector for several partners. This includes the predictions of mineralisations all over the world. This dataset is described in more detail in section 7.5.

5.3.1. Fabricated Data

Since we work with explicit models it is very unlikely that we are able describe the underlying ground truth perfectly. However, the procedure should be able to detect the ground truth if possible and if it is not possible it should at least detect parts of the ground truth. Furthermore, it would be desirable to have some measure of the importance of the variables in the final model such that the user is able to discern which variables might belong to the ground truth. We develop and test the method on two different fabricated datasets that differ in their non-linearity. Both datasets are composed of 30 variables that are drawn from a standard univariate normal density. For all variables included in the model we set the parameters $\beta_j = 1, j = 1, \ldots, \tilde{m}$, where $\tilde{m}$ denotes the total number of variables including all non-linearities. The intercept β_0 is chosen such that the percentage of positive target events is approximately 1%. We then generate $n = 10^6$ observations from the given logistic regression model. For each observation i we drew a random number r and assigned $y_i = 1$ if $\mu_i > r$ and $y_i = 0$ otherwise. The dataset at the beginning of the model selection procedure consists of the matrix $X \in \mathbb{R}^{10^6 \times 30}$ and the vector $y \in \mathbb{R}^{10^6}$ of all targets.

Data with little non-linearity - fab1

The ground truth of this dataset consists of a total of 21 variables plus the intercept. This involves 15 covariates, 3 squares and 3 two-fold interactions of those variables involved:

- x_1 to x_{15},

- x_2^2, x_8^2, x_{12}^2,

- $x_4 : x_7$, $x_6 : x_{14}$, $x_9 : x_{13}$.

We will refer to this dataset as "fab1". This dataset is fairly simple, and the model selection should be able to detect this model.

Data with intermediate non-linearity - fab2

To check the performance of the procedure on data it can only partly recover we use the dataset "fab2". This involves the same 15 covariables as in "fab1". In addition, there are 2 squares and 3 two-fold interactions that, potentially, can be recovered. Additional non-linearities involve 2 three-fold interactions, 2 four-fold interactions and 1 two-fold interaction between two squares:

- x_1 to x_{15},

- x_5^2, x_{11}^2,

- $x_1 : x_3$, $x_7 : x_{10}$, $x_{12} : x_{15}$,

- $x_2 : x_8 : x_{15}$, $x_4 : x_{13} : x_{14}$,

- $x_3 : x_5 : x_9 : x_{13}$, $x_2 : x_8 : x_9 : x_{20}$,

- $x_1^2 : x_{10}^2$.

Thus, the model selection should be able to detect the 20 variables it can recover plus the intercept. The other 5 variables that cannot be detected might be approximated through the selection of other variables.

5.3.2. Real World Data

The datasets are selected such that they match a possible dataset from prospectivity modeling: They only have a small fraction of positive target events. Furthermore, they have a lot of samples compared to the number of predictor variables. An overview of the datasets is given in Table 5.1.

The ds1.10 and ds1.100 datasets are taken from [36] and are from the same compressed life sciences dataset. Each row of the original ds1 dataset represents a chemistry or biology experiment, and the output represents the reactivity of the compound observed in the experiment. The full ds1 dataset consists of 6348 binary features. The authors in [36] created the two datasets ds1.10 and ds1.100 using a principal component analysis. Thereby only the top 10 and top 100 principal components are used for ds1.10 and ds1.100, respectively. The features are now real valued.

The forest covertype dataset is also from [22] and contains cartographic variables as covariates and the output is the forest cover type which is divided into seven categories. We took category three to be our target and considered all other categories as non-targets. A datapoint covers an area of $30m \times 30m$. Furthermore, we only considered the ten real valued variables and did not include the 44 binary covariables that are constructed from categorical variables. This is necessary because we did not consider grouped variable selection in our suggested procedure yet.

The Cod-RNA dataset is taken from [60]. The covariates are predicted secondary structure formation free energy changes. The targets to be classified are non-coding RNAs. The Cod-RNA dataset was randomly sampled such that the target event has an occurrence of 5%.

Gold Mineralisations in Ghana

The Ghana dataset was provided by Beak Consultants GmbH, Freiberg, Germany. The dataset describes geochemical, geological, geophysical and tectonic data from a survey area in Ghana. The target variable of interest is gold. A more precise description of the data is given in section 7.5.

	Instances	Covariates	Class		Rarity(%)
			0	1	
ds1.10	26 733	10	25 929	804	3
ds1.100	26 733	100	25 929	804	3
Covertype	581 012	10	545 258	35 754	6.6
Cod-RNA	220 779	8	209 740	11 039	5
Ghana	6 091 636	30	6 055 475	36 161	0.1

Tab. 5.1.: Overview of the real world datasets.

5.4. Evaluation Metrics

After the model selection is finished the resulting model needs to be validated on unseen data in order to show its ability to make predictions. At the same time this can be used to compare the procedure to other methods. This can be done by using a contingency matrix, also called confusion matrix. Usually the cutoff is chosen as 0.5, meaning all predicted values smaller than 0.5 are assigned to the negative class and all predicted values equal or greater than 0.5 are assigned to the positive class. The confusion matrix reads

$$
\begin{array}{r}
\text{actual positive (AP)} \\
\text{actual negative (AN)}
\end{array}
\begin{pmatrix}
\text{true positive (TP)} & \text{false negative (FN)} \\
\text{false positive (FP)} & \text{true negative (TN)}
\end{pmatrix}
$$

with true positive (TP) describing the number of cases 1 correctly classified as 1, false positive (FP) describing the number of cases 0 incorrectly classified as 1, true negative (TN) describing the number of cases 0 correctly classified as 0 and false negative (FN) describing the number of cases 1 incorrectly classified as 0.

A very common measure is the accuracy which describes the ratio of correctly classified cases to misclassified cases. This can be further divided into true positive rate TPR, also called recall, (fraction of cases 1 correctly classified) and true negative rate TNR (fraction of cases 0 correctly classified). Furthermore, we use the precision PREC (fraction of truly predicted cases 1 to all predicted cases 1) as a measure. The measures are calculated as

- $\text{Accuracy} = \frac{TP+TN}{FP+FN}$

- $TPR = \frac{TP}{AP} = \frac{TP}{TP+FN} = 1 - FNR$

- $TNR = \frac{TN}{AN} = \frac{TN}{TN+FP} = 1 - FPR$

- $PREC = \frac{TP}{TP+FP}$

- $FPR = \frac{FP}{AN} = \frac{FP}{FP+TN}$

5.4.1. The Wrong Scoring Metric

Comparing different classification algorithms in terms of prediction ability is often done using the receiver operating characteristic curve (ROC-curve). The x-axis of the ROC-curve denotes the FPR whereas the y-axis denotes the TPR. To put it simply, it shows the fraction of false

positive predicted cases compared to the fraction of true positive predicted cases. An example
of a ROC-curve is shown in Figure 5.7.

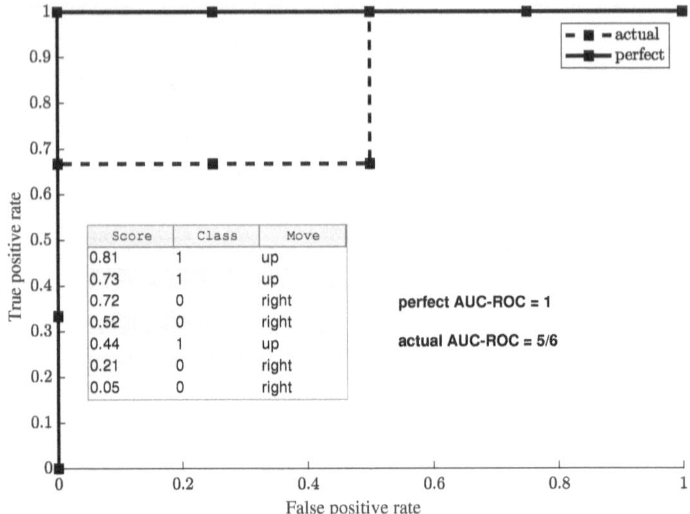

Fig. 5.7.: Example ROC-curve.

The ROC-curve shows the relationship of TPR with FPR for every cutoff between zero
and one. To construct it one sorts the predicted scores for every experiment from largest to
smallest. Starting with the largest score one takes a step up or right when the experiment has
a positive target or negative target, respectively. The ROC-curve always starts in $(0, 0)$ and
ends in $(1, 1)$. The perfect classifier would first go up to 1 on the y-axis and only then go to
the right until it reaches 1 on the x-axis. This means all positive targets have a larger score
than any negative target. Random classification in turn would result in a diagonal line. To
summarize the prediction ability in one value the area under the ROC-curve, called AUROC,
is used. As the name suggests this is simply the area that is under the ROC-curve. Hence the
perfect classifier has an AUROC of 1 and a random classifier has an AUROC of 0.5.

Since we consider the rare event case the accuracy does not provide a satisfying measure
to evaluate the performance of classification methods. For example, consider the confusion
matrix

$$
\begin{array}{c}
\\
\text{actual positive (AP)} \\
\text{actual negative (AN)}
\end{array}
\begin{array}{cc}
\text{predicted positive (PP)} & \text{predicted negative (PN)} \\
\left(\begin{array}{cc}
90 & 10 \\
100.000 & 900.000
\end{array} \right) .
\end{array}
\tag{5.1}
$$

The classifier producing this confusion matrix yields 90% for TPR and TNR and therefore
an accuracy of 90%. This would also give a fairly good looking ROC-curve since we reach 0.9
on the y-axis before when we reach 0.11 on the x-axis. However, the precision is only about
0.09%. Thus only 0.09% of the predicted locations actually contain a mineralisation which
basically makes this method useless for practical applications.

5.4.2. The Right Scoring Metric

When dealing with rare events it is better to use the precision-recall-curve (PR-curve) [19].
The PR-curve describes the relation of precision to true positive rate. A perfect classifier

would start at $(0,1)$ and go to the right towards $(1,1)$ before dropping to $(1, \bar{y})$. A random classifier would be a straight line at $y = \bar{y}$.

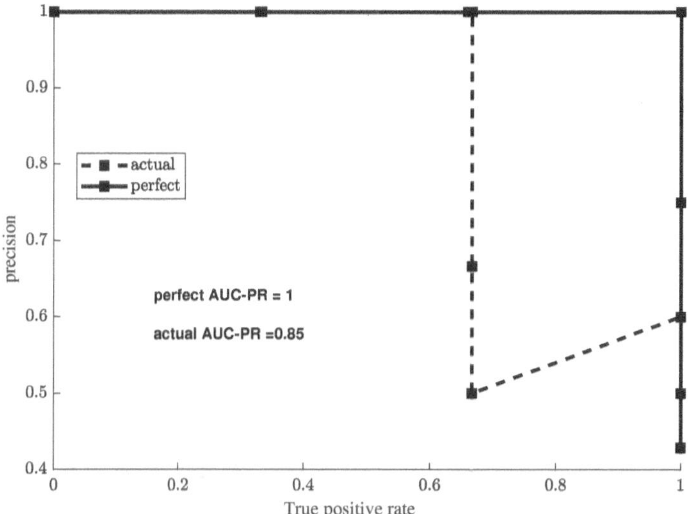

Fig. 5.8.: Example PR-curve.

The advantage of the PR-curve is that it is independent on the number of negative examples. It rewards a smaller recall range with higher precision. Based on the example given in [19] we show the result of two classifiers on the same dataset in the ROC-space and in PR-space in Figure 5.9. The dataset consists of 1000 datapoints of which only 20 belong to the positive class. In ROC-space they show similar performance. Classifier 2 even has a slightly higher AUROC score than classifier 1. So based on this metric the user would select classifier 2 as the preferred one. However, in PR-space the difference is indisputable with classifier 2 being the better one by far. Although both spaces show different results regarding the quality of a classifier there is a one-to-one mapping between points in ROC space and PR space. Hence, a curve in ROC space can be translated in PR space and vice-versa. Furthermore, it is proved in [19] that one curve dominates a second curve in ROC space if and only if it dominates the second curve in PR space. Hereby a curve is said to dominate another curve if all points of that other curve are beneath or equal to the points of the first curve.

Furthermore, we use the $F1$-score which is a summary statistic for TPR and PREC and is calculated as

$$F_1 = 2 \cdot \frac{\text{TPR} \cdot \text{PREC}}{\text{TPR} + \text{PREC}}.$$

This balances the two measures. A large F_1-score indicates that the classifier exhibits a high TPR as well as a high PREC.

5.5. Computing Platform

We used a single computing platform for all experiments of this book. The platform is equipped with 4 AMD Opteron 6136 processors (2.4 Ghz), where each processor has 8 cores. The machine has a total of 256 GB of main memory and is running GNU/Linux. No computation was performed in parallel. We used MATLAB R2020a.

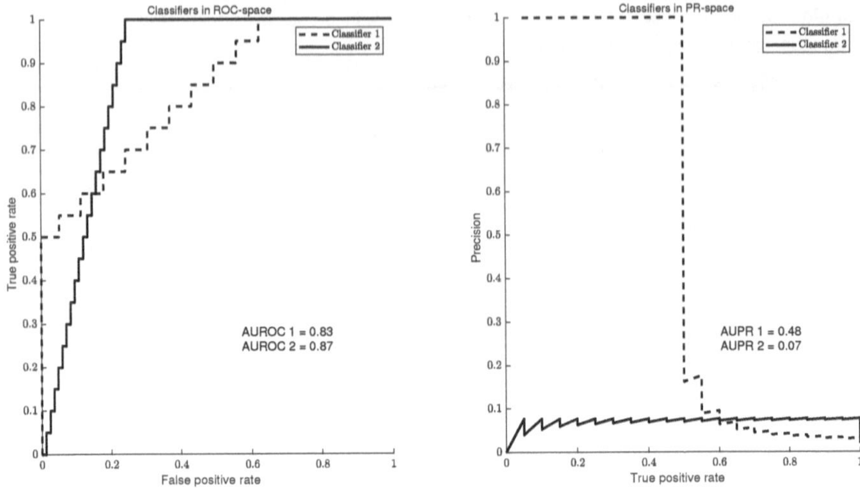

Fig. 5.9.: Two classifiers in ROC-space and in PR-space with corresponding AUC scores. Classifier 1 seems to be better in ROC-space. However, in PR-space classifier 2 is better making it more adequate for rare events.

5.6. Scope

In the following chapter we develop a model selection procedure adjusted for rare events. The overall goal is to provide an interpretable model to the user. On the one hand this means to detect the ground truth when it is in the domain of the model.

On the other hand the provided model should contain that part of the ground truth that lies in the domain. It might furthermore add other variables to approximate non-linearities that are outside its domain to improve the classification on unseen data. A desirable property of the procedure is to have some measure for the importance of the variables of the final model, i.e. distinguish between variables that are potentially part of the ground truth and variables that are included to improve classification. In forward selection one can conclude that variables that entered the model earlier are more important than the ones entering later. However, it is hard to tell which of those variables might belong to the ground truth and which are just for improving the classification. With our approach we also provide some helpful guidance for the researcher.

6. Model Selection for Rare Events Logistic Regression

In this chapter, we develop our proposed model selection procedure. As described earlier there are several methods available for model selection. Our approach aims to automate to some extend the purposeful selection described in section 4.7. We aim to take the researcher out of the model building process. We are well aware that this will not replace the expert. However this automated selection might help to save time and resources. The final models can then be taken under detailed examination by the researcher who hopefully can draw some conclusion.

6.1. Main Idea

The main idea is to start with a full model including all possible interactions and non-linearities that are selected to be potentially part of the model and then perform the backward selection of significant variables in two main parts. In the first part we use the Wald statistic to eliminate the majority of insignificant variables. In the second part the elimination is conducted more carefully using the Bayes' information criterion (BIC). However simply putting together these two parts will not work. The progress of the development of our proposed WBIC method will be examined in section 6.2

6.1.1. Part I: Wald statistic

In order to use the Wald statistic in our setting an adjustment for the covariance matrix needs to be applied. As described in [62], if the parameters are heteroscedastic, i.e. their variance is not equal, the calculation of the variance matrix is inefficient. This is also the case when the model is misspecified. They propose a correction for linear models. In the case of generalized linear models such as logistic regression, [34] describe the corrected estimate for the variance, also called sandwich estimate, as

$$V(\beta) = \boldsymbol{P}^{-1}\boldsymbol{M}\boldsymbol{P}^{-1} \tag{6.1}$$

with $\boldsymbol{P} = \mathbb{E}(\nabla^2 \ln \mathbb{L}(\boldsymbol{\beta}))$, the expectation of the Hessian, and $\boldsymbol{M} = \mathbb{V}(\nabla \ln \mathbb{L}(\boldsymbol{\beta}))$, the covariance of the gradient. Even with the sandwich estimator, there are some known issues concerning the p-value of the Wald statistic as a measure of variable importance. On the one hand it tends to zero for large samples [39]. This means that increasing the sample size while maintaining the current model, every parameter will become significant eventually. As shown in [39] this can start for sample sizes of about 2000. On the other hand [31] reported that even when the coefficient was significant the Wald test often failed to reject the null hypothesis. These two problems act in different directions in the sense that the one tends to leave too many variables in the model and the other that it may fail to leave important variables in the model. This needs to be taken into consideration when using the Wald statistic as part of our model selection strategy.

Despite these possible shortcomings we use the Wald test for part 1 of our model selection. It is possible to reject several variables at once without computing the MLE for every case. There are basically two hyperparameters that can be adjusted, i.e. parameters that control the learning. The first one is the value of the regularization parameter λ and the second one is the threshold α_R for the p-value which is used to decide whether the variable should remain in the model or should be removed. We conduct different experiments in order to find some fixed values for both hyperparameters such that the user does not need to experiment with different values himself.

6.1.2. Part II: Bayes' Information Criterion

For the fine selection of our procedure we use the BIC, defined as in equation (4.15). We did try the AIC but as described in the literature the AIC tends to include too many variables in the model [23]. Hence we do not report results using the AIC. Let $\mathcal{N}$ be the set of variables that are identified to be not important. We denote with BIC_0 the BIC value of the current model. In the same way let BIC_j denote the BIC value of the current model without variable j. We then calculate the difference between the current model and the one without variable j, i.e.

$$d_j = \mathrm{BIC}_0 - \mathrm{BIC}_j. \tag{6.2}$$

Since a smaller value of the information criterion indicates a favorable model, all variables with $d_j > 0$ are considered to be eliminated since the model without this variable is better in terms of the BIC.

6.2. Development of the Final Procedure WBIC

We will start with the naive approach as version 1 and improve it several times until we end with version 4 which is the final version of WBIC. For every version we give the pseudo-code and its update as we proceed. The changes made will be indicated with red. The improvements are made through theoretical considerations and are compared to each other regarding the performance using the two datasets fab1 and fab2. The final assessment of the procedure is the comparison with other methods on real world datasets. The datasets are divided into training set (80%) and test set (20%). This is done before the model selection starts, i.e. the sampling is only performed on the training data. The test set is only used for testing the performance of the selected models on unseen data. This is important to evaluate the ability to replace variables that are out of the scope of the model with variables that improve the prediction ability. Sampling from the training data such that the fraction of positive events is $\bar{y} = 0.33$ leads to approximately $n_s = 3700$ examples in both fab1 and fab2. Furthermore, as a reference for computation time and the ability to select the true variables we use the *stepwiseglm* from the statistical toolbox in MATLAB. It uses forward selection and is able to also incorporate non-linearities in the logit. In the settings for *stepwiseglm* we choose to fit a model potentially using a full quadratic logit. This enables the function to select squares and two-fold interactions and is thus directly comparable to our approach. All other settings are chosen as default. This includes using the likelihood ratio test to decide whether a variable should enter the model. The threshold of the p-value for entering is 0.05, meaning the variable enters the model if the p-value of the likelihood ratio test is less than 0.05. In addition, after a variable entered the model, all variable are analyzed for a potential removal from the model. This happens if the p-value of a variable for the likelihood ratio test exceeds 0.1.

We use *stepwiseglm* twice, once on the full training data ($\approx 1\%$ pos. events) and once on the sampled data ($\approx 33\%$ pos. events). The baseline results of the two *stepwiseglm* variants are given in Table 6.1. This table is continuously updated for every new version of our procedure. Every version is executed ten times except *stepwiseglm* full which is executed only once since there is no variation in the data through sampling. The values given in the tables are the mean values of all runs.

Both version were able to detect all true variables in fab1 as well as fab2. However around six additional variables are present in the final model for fab1. Interestingly, the additional

	fab1			fab2		
	Time(s)	Num Var	True Var	Time(s)	Num Var	True Var
stepwiseglm sampled	1 918	28.8	22	4 714	50.8	21
stepwiseglm full	65 227	28	22	290 888	69	21

Tab. 6.1.: In dataset fab1 the methods should detect all 22 truly involved variables. Since no other non-linearity is present in the ground truth that should also be the total number of variables. In dataset fab2 the methods should detect all 21 truly involved variables. Some more might be found to approximate other non-linearities present in the ground truth.

variables selected in the sampled version of *stepwiseglm* do not coincide with the ones selected in the full data approach. For fab2 the number of additional variables is even higher. The *stepwiseglm* method on the full data took around 50 times longer than for the sampled data. Here, the MATLAB routine *stepwiseglm* uses shared-memory-parallelism.

6.3. Version 1: The Naive Model Selection

The first version is the naive approach simply putting the two parts together using Wald statistic and BIC as explained in section 6.1. In the first part we choose the default value $\alpha_R = 0.2$ as threshold for the p-value in the Wald statistic as suggested in [32]. We remove every variable with a p-value above that threshold and repeat the procedure until all remaining variables exhibit a p-value smaller than α_R. In the second part we use the BIC, calculate the d_j and simply remove the variable with the largest d_j. This is repeated as long as none of the variables have $d_j > 0$. For the regularization parameter we start with $\lambda = 1$. Version 1 is formalized in pseudo code in Algorithm 1 and 2.

Algorithm 1 Part 1.v1: Wald statistic

Initialize $\alpha_R = 0.2, \mathcal{N} = \mathcal{I}, \lambda = 1$
while $\mathcal{N} \neq \emptyset$ **do**
    Calculate MLE $\hat{\beta}$ via (4.50) using all variables $j \in \mathcal{I}$
    Calculate p-values for all parameters β_j via (6.1)
    Update $\mathcal{N} = \{j | p_j \geq \alpha\}, \mathcal{I} = \mathcal{I} \backslash \mathcal{N}$
end while
return $\mathcal{I}$

The mean values of this approach are depicted in Table 6.2. The first naive attempt, simply combining the Wald statistic and the BIC did incorporate the true variables in the final model. However, it selected a large number of unimportant variables for both fab1 and fab2. Even though it was faster than *stepwiseglm* on the full data, it took over ten times longer for fab1 and four times longer for fab2 than *stepwiseglm* sampled. As it turns out, the first part of the procedure does only take about 13 seconds. In order to reduce the computational cost we need to optimize the second part. After part one there are approximately 150 remaining variable for fab1. Hence the second part eliminated around 65 variables. This implies a total of roughly

$$\frac{(149 - 85 + 1)(149 + 85)}{2} = \frac{65 \cdot 234}{2} = 7605$$

LR model fits. This leads to the long computation time although a single LR model fit only takes about three seconds. The conclusion of the first attempt is that we need to change part

Algorithm 2 Part 2.v1: Bayes' Information Criterion

Initialize $\mathcal{N} = \mathcal{I}, \lambda = 1$
while $\mathcal{N} \neq \emptyset$ **do**
    Calculate BIC_0 of current model via (4.15)
    for $j \in \mathcal{I}$ **do**
        Calculate BIC_j as BIC of model without variable j
        Calculate $d_j = \text{BIC}_0 - \text{BIC}_j$
    end for
    $\mathcal{N} = \{l \mid d_l = \max_{j \in \mathcal{I}} d_j \quad \textbf{and} \quad d_l > 0\}$
    $\mathcal{I} = \mathcal{I} \backslash \mathcal{N}$
end while
return $\mathcal{I}$

---

	fab1			fab2		
	Time(s)	Num Var	True Var	Time(s)	Num Var	True Var
stepwiseglm sampled	1 918	28.8	22	4 714	50.8	21
stepwiseglm full	65 227	28	22	290 888	69	21
WBIC - version 1	24 954	86	22	16 742	133.5	21

Tab. 6.2.: In dataset fab1 the methods should detect all 22 truly involved variables. Since no other non-linearity is present in the ground truth that should also be the total number of variables. In dataset fab2 the methods should detect all 21 truly involved variables. Some more might be found to approximate other non-linearities present in the ground truth.

2 in order to speed things up.

6.4. Version 2: Speeding Things Up

We survey the sorted BIC values after the first iteration of part 2. Their sorted values are shown in Figure 6.1.

Both plots exhibit the same structure. There are some variables that have a very small d_j meaning they are rated to be very important. But there is also a long tail of variables with d_j slightly smaller than zero and slightly greater than zero. Both datasets have around 90 variables that are rated to be not important, i.e. having $d_j > 0$. This raises the question whether one could remove more than just the one variable with the largest d_j per iteration. This assumes that no important variable exhibits a value $d_j > 0$ because this makes it prone to being removed. We introduce a stepwise-like variant in the BIC based variable removal. We define the set $\mathcal{D} = \{j \in \mathcal{I} | d_j > 0\}$ which is sorted in descending order, i.e. $d_j > d_k$ for $j < k$. We then consider three different subsets of $\mathcal{D}$, namely

- $\mathcal{D}_{\frac{1}{2}} = \{j \in \mathcal{D} | j < \frac{|\mathcal{D}|}{2}\}$,

- $\mathcal{D}_{\frac{1}{4}} = \{j \in \mathcal{D} | j < \frac{|\mathcal{D}|}{4}\}$,

- $\mathcal{D}_{\frac{1}{8}} = \{j \in \mathcal{D} | j < \frac{|\mathcal{D}|}{8}\}$,

where $|\mathcal{D}|$ denotes the total number of elements in $\mathcal{D}$. Afterwards three LR models are fitted, one for every set of variables $\mathcal{I} \backslash \mathcal{D}_{1/q}, q = 2, 4, 8$. The three corresponding BIC values $\text{BIC}_{1/q}$

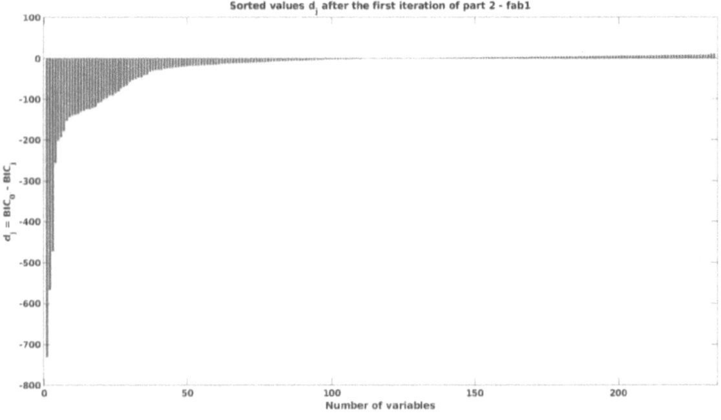

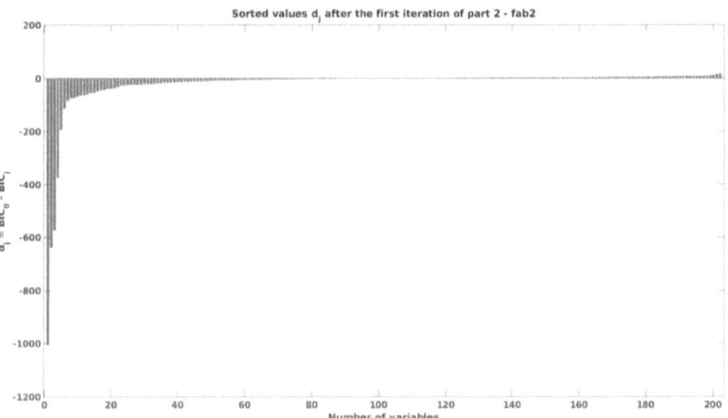

Fig. 6.1.: The sorted values d_j for fab1 and fab2 after the first iteration of part 2. Variables with $d_j < 0$ are rated to be important and Variables with $d_j > 0$ are rated to be unimportant. The larger the absolute value of d_j the more important or unimportant is the variable compared to other variables, respectively.

as well as their values $d_{1/q} = \mathrm{BIC}_0 - \mathrm{BIC}_{1/q}, q = 2, 4, 8$, are calculated. The variables of $\mathcal{D}_{1/q}$ corresponding to the model with the largest value $d_{1/q} > 0$ are removed in this iteration. If no value d is greater than zero, the variable selection ends.

We apply another change in part 1. Instead of choosing $\alpha_R = 0.2$ right at the beginning we choose a rather larger threshold of $\alpha_R = 0.7$. In addition, we introduce a final threshold $\alpha_E = 0.2$. Starting with $\alpha_R = 0.7$, we remove all variables with p-values greater than α_R. After each iteration, we update $\alpha_R = \alpha_R - 0.1$ until we reach the final threshold α_E. With $\alpha_R = \alpha_E$ we proceed as long as there exist variables with a p-value greater than α_R. We found that this stepwise reduction of the threshold somehow stabilizes the number of final variables after part 1. The updated method is formalized in Algorithm 3 and 4.

The results of the executing of version 2 of the model selection for fab1 and fab2 are summa-

---

Algorithm 3 Part 1.v2: Wald statistic

Initialize $\alpha_R = 0.7, \alpha_E = 0.2, \mathcal{N} = \mathcal{I}, \lambda = 1$
while $\mathcal{N} \neq \emptyset$ or $\alpha_R > \alpha_E$ **do**
    Calculate MLE $\hat{\beta}$ via (4.50) using all variables $j \in \mathcal{I}$
    Calculate p-values for all parameters β_j via (6.1)
    Update $\mathcal{N} = \{j | p_j \geq \alpha_R\}$, $\mathcal{I} = \mathcal{I} \backslash \mathcal{N}$
    $\alpha_R = \max(\alpha_R - 0.1, \alpha_E)$
end while
return $\mathcal{I}$

Algorithm 4 Part 2.v2: Bayes' Information Criterion

Initialize $\mathcal{N} = \mathcal{I}, \lambda = \lambda_1$
while $\mathcal{N} \neq \emptyset$ **do**
    Calculate BIC_0 of current model via (4.15)
    for $j \in \mathcal{I}$ **do**
        Calculate BIC_j as BIC of model without variable j
        Calculate $d_j = \mathrm{BIC}_0 - \mathrm{BIC}_j$
    end for
    Calculate $\mathrm{BIC}_{1/q}$ for $q = 2, 4, 8$
    if $\min \mathrm{BIC}_{1/q} < \mathrm{BIC}_0$ **then**
        Choose model that yield minimum BIC
        $\mathcal{N} = \mathcal{N}_{1/q}$
    else
        $\mathcal{N} = \emptyset$
    end if
    $\mathcal{I} = \mathcal{I} \backslash \mathcal{N}$
end while
return $\mathcal{I}$

---

rized in Table 6.3.

	fab1			fab2		
	Time(s)	Num Var	True Var	Time(s)	Num Var	True Var
stepwiseglm sampled	1 918	28.8	22	4 714	50.8	21
stepwiseglm full	65 227	28	22	290 888	69	21
WBIC - version 1	24 954	86	22	16 742	133.5	21
WBIC - version 2	2 856	83	22	3 452	131.6	21

Tab. 6.3.: In dataset fab1 the methods should detect all 22 truly involved variables. Since no other non-linearity is present in the ground truth that should also be the total number of variables. In dataset fab2 the methods should detect all 21 truly involved variables. Some more might be found to approximate other non-linearities present in the ground truth.

These changes speed up the procedure by an order of magnitude. We did come closer to *stepwiseglm* sampled in terms of speed. The final variables selected do not differ much compared to version 1. The procedure does still select all true variables but does also still select a lot of unimportant variables. The problem of removing unimportant variables is tackled in the next section.

6.5. Version 3: Reduce Number of Unimportant Variables

Removing more than one variable per iteration in the second part of the model selection did improve the speed drastically. To address the issue of too many variables we investigate the final values d_j of the variables after the model selection finished. The sorted values are shown in Figure 6.2 for fab1 and fab2.

Again there is a long tail of variables whose removal would degrade the model only slightly in terms of the BIC (note the logarithmic y-scale). One could change the threshold for the variables d_j from zero to some negative number. But first of all is it difficult to determine a particular number without knowing which variables might actually contribute for a better classification result. Second, this would also neglect the theory behind the BIC.

The red bars in Figure 6.2 correspond to the true variables. While a possible point to cut off the long tail is pretty obvious for fab1 it is not so obvious any more for fab2. This is because a lot of variables that are not part of the true model become more important for approximating terms that are not in the scope of the model selection procedure. The two variables with the largest absolute values are x_1^2 and x_{10}^2. They are not part of the true model itself but contribute through their two-fold interaction $x_1^2 x_{10}^2$.

One could interpret the selection of too many variables from the training data as overfitting. Although for the BIC the probability of selecting the true model will approach one as the sample size increases this is not a realistic setting for real world data. There is no way to increase the sample size of the data in applications. Especially in the rare event case our sample might not contain much data. Another point to consider is that the model selection itself is performed on sampled data. In this sampled data the ratio of positive to negative events is not unbalanced (1 : 2 in our case). Although we apply all corrections described earlier for the calculation of the MLE it is not clear whether this arbitrarily large fraction of positive events might interfere with the importance of variables. This leads to the idea to approximate the effect of removing a variable on the rare data the model is supposed

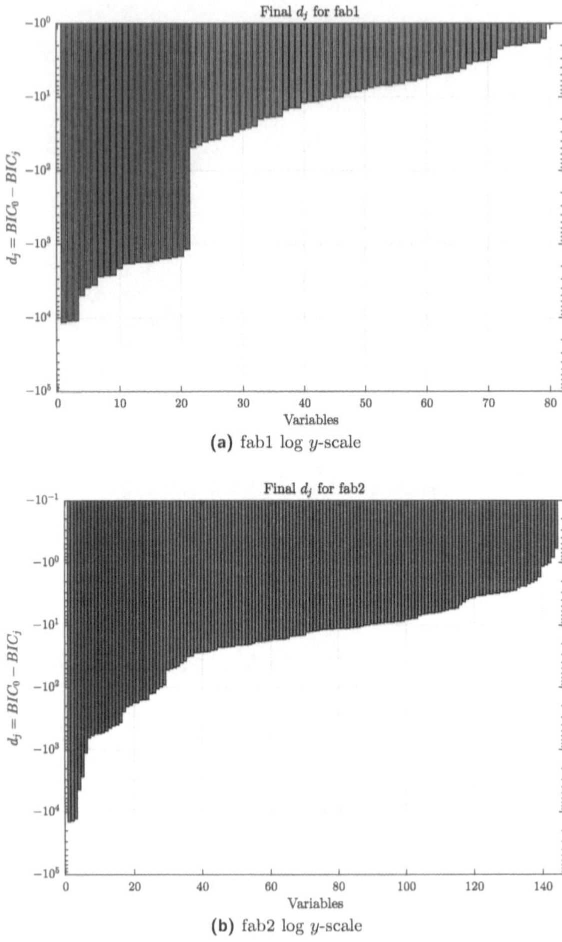

(a) fab1 log y-scale

(b) fab2 log y-scale

Fig. 6.2.: BIC summary after last iteration for (a) fab1 and (b) fab2. The red values correspond to the true variables. Note the logarithmic y-scale.

to describe in the first place. Hence, we introduce a new dataset which we call validation data. Thus instead of using 80% of the full dataset as training data, we now only use 60% as training data and the remaining 20% as validation data. The validation data is not sampled and therewith reflects the true fraction of positive events in the data.

Version 3 of the model selection is now defined as follows. In part 2 we fit the model on the sampled training data as before. But now instead of calculating the value of the BIC on this sampled data we use the MLE estimate $\hat{\beta}$ of the current model to calculate the value of the BIC using the validation data. We then remove a variable and fit the model without this variable using the sampled data. We use the calculated MLE to get the BIC value using the validation data. This is performed for all variables in the model. Afterwards we proceed as before creating three different models and choosing the one with the largest difference d to be the new model. This is repeated until no variable can be removed without worsening the BIC. The updates of the procedure are formalized in Algorithm 5 and 6.

Algorithm 5 Part 1.v3: Wald statistic

Initialize $\alpha_R = 0.7, \alpha_E = 0.2, \mathcal{N} = \mathcal{I}, \lambda = 1$
while $\mathcal{N} \neq \emptyset$ **or** $\alpha_R > \alpha_E$ **do**
    Calculate MLE $\hat{\beta}$ via (4.50) using all variables $j \in \mathcal{I}$
    Calculate p-values for all parameters β_j via (6.1)
    Update $\mathcal{N} = \{j > m + 1 | p_j \geq \alpha_R\}$, $\mathcal{I} = \mathcal{I} \backslash \mathcal{N}$
    $\alpha_R = \max(\alpha_R - 0.1, \alpha_E)$
end while
return $\mathcal{I}$

Algorithm 6 Part 2.v3: Bayes' Information Criterion

Initialize $\mathcal{N} = \mathcal{I}, \lambda = \lambda_1$
while $\mathcal{N} \neq \emptyset$ **do**
    Calculate the MLE of the current model via (4.50) using all variables $j \in \mathcal{I}$
    Calculate BIC_0 of current model using the validation set $\boldsymbol{X}_{val}$ via (4.15)
    for $j \in \mathcal{I}$ **do**
        Calculate BIC_j as BIC of model without variable j using $\boldsymbol{X}_{val}$
        Calculate $d_j = \text{BIC}_0 - \text{BIC}_j$
    end for
    Calculate $\text{BIC}_{1/q}$ for $q = 2, 4, 8$ using $\boldsymbol{X}_{val}$
    if $\min \text{BIC}_{1/q} < \text{BIC}_0$ **then**
        Choose model that yield minimum BIC
        $\mathcal{N} = \mathcal{N}_{1/q}$
    else
        $\mathcal{N} = \emptyset$
    end if
    $\mathcal{I} = \mathcal{I} \backslash \mathcal{N}$
end while
return $\mathcal{I}$

The results for this new procedure is shown in Table 6.4.

On dataset fab1 our procedure is almost 40% faster than *stepwiseglm* sampled. Furthermore, it finds the true model in every of the ten runs without selecting a single additional variable. This suggests that the procedure is able to detect the ground truth as long as it is part of the scope of the model. On fab2 the model selection is even 80% faster than *stepwiseglm* sampled. The goal of this section is also reached as there are only 7 variables selected that are not part of the ground truth. However, we loose one true variable on average. A remedy to this problem is given in the last update of the method.

6.6. Version 4: Final Version

An analysis of the time when the true variables are removed from the model showed that this happens quite early in the BIC selection part. Furthermore, the procedure happens to remove a covariate rather than an interaction. The removal of a covariate might result in a value $d_j > 0$. This can happen if the square or an interaction involving this variable is also present in the model and has a similar effect as the variable itself. If this difference is large

	fab1			fab2		
	Time(s)	Num Var	True Var	Time(s)	Num Var	True Var
stepwiseglm sampled	1 918	28.8	22	4 714	50.8	21
stepwiseglm full	65 227	28	22	290 888	69	21
WBIC - version 1	24 954	86	22	16 742	133.5	21
WBIC - version 2	2 856	83	22	3 452	131.6	21
WBIC - version 3	1 233	22	22	949	26.6	19.9

Tab. 6.4.: In dataset fab1 the methods should detect all 22 truly involved variables. Since no other non-linearity is present in the ground truth that should also be the total number of variables. In dataset fab2 the methods should detect all 21 truly involved variables. Some more might be found to approximate other non-linearities present in the ground truth.

enough for the variable to be in the set $\mathcal{D}_{\frac{1}{2}}$ it can be removed since the removal of a lot of unimportant variables at the same time still improves the BIC value of the resulting model.

Hence, as a last change, we apply the BIC based removal of variables not to the whole set of variables at once but use groups of variables. We stress again that the overall goal is still a model that is as simple as possible while having still good classification abilities. So it seems natural to first remove complicated terms if they are not beneficial for the BIC value. The removal of unimportant complicated terms will then result in a larger importance of remaining variables in the model. Formalizing this approach we introduce different groups of variables grouped together by their complexity. The different groups are saved in sets:

i) $G_1 = \{j \in \mathcal{I} \mid x_j \text{ is covariate}\}$

ii) $G_2 = \{j \in \mathcal{I} \mid x_j \text{ is square of covariate}\}$

iii) $G_3 = \{j \in \mathcal{I} \mid x_j \text{ is two-fold interaction or higher order non-linearity}\}$

The set G_3 is defined since the procedure allows for more complexity in the logit as long as there are enough samples in the data. This set is added later using real world data to see if the procedure can detect more true variables or improve the classification.

After performing the removal in every group one after another a final BIC value check is performed for all remaining variables removing the variables that are now not important in terms of their BIC value one by one. The final algorithm is formalized in Algorithm 7 and 8.

Algorithm 7 Part 1.v4: Wald statistic

Initialize $\alpha_R = 0.7, \alpha_E = 0.2, \mathcal{N} = \mathcal{I}, \lambda = 1$
while $\mathcal{N} \neq \emptyset$ **or** $\alpha_R > \alpha_E$ **do**
   Calculate MLE $\hat{\beta}$ via (4.50) using all variables $j \in \mathcal{I}$
   Calculate p-values for all parameters β_j via (6.1)
   Update $\mathcal{N} = \{j > m + 1 \mid p_j \geq \alpha_R\}, \mathcal{I} = \mathcal{I} \backslash \mathcal{N}$
   $\alpha_R = \max(\alpha_R - 0.1, \alpha_E)$
end while
return $\mathcal{I}$

The mean result of 10 runs of the new version is shown in the updated Table 6.5. The variable

---
Algorithm 8 Part 2.v4: Bayes' Information Criterion

Initialize $\mathcal{N} = \mathcal{I}$, $\lambda = \lambda_1$
while $i = n : -1 : 0$ **do**
  if $i == 0$ **then**
    $\mathcal{S} = \mathcal{I}$
  else
    $\mathcal{S} = G_i$
  end if
  while $\mathcal{N} \neq \emptyset$ **do**
    Calculate the MLE of the current model
    Calculate BIC_0 of current model using the validation set $\boldsymbol{X}_{val}$ via (4.15)
    for $j \in \mathcal{S}$ **do**
      Calculate BIC_j as BIC of model without variable j using $\boldsymbol{X}_{val}$
      Calculate $d_j = \text{BIC}_0 - \text{BIC}_j$
    end for
    Calculate $\text{BIC}_{1/q}$ for $q = 2, 4, 8$ using $\boldsymbol{X}_{val}$
    if $\min \text{BIC}_{1/q} < \text{BIC}_0$ **then**
      Choose model that yield minimum BIC
      $\mathcal{N} = \mathcal{N}_{1/q}$
    else
      $\mathcal{N} = \emptyset$
    end if
    $\mathcal{I} = \mathcal{I} \backslash \mathcal{N}$
  end while
end while
return $\mathcal{I}$

Algorithm 9 Final WBIC model selection approach

Choose the set $\mathcal{I}$ as scope of the model
Create $\boldsymbol{X}_{val}$ and $\boldsymbol{X}_{train}$
Perform endogenous sampling to obtain $\boldsymbol{X}_s, \boldsymbol{y}_s$
Apply algorithm 7 to update the set $\mathcal{I}$
Apply algorithm 8 to obtain final model with variables $\mathcal{I}$

---

	fab1			fab2		
	Time(s)	Num Var	True Var	Time(s)	Num Var	True Var
stepwiseglm sampled	1 918	28.8	22	4 714	50.8	21
stepwiseglm full	65 227	28	22	290 888	69	21
WBIC - version 1	24 954	86	22	16 742	133.5	21
WBIC - version 2	2 856	83	22	3 452	131.6	21
WBIC - version 3	1 233	22	22	949	26.6	19.9
WBIC - version 4	1 141	22	22	907	26.8	20.9

Tab. 6.5.: In dataset fab1 the methods should detect all 22 truly involved variables. Since no other non-linearity is present in the ground truth that should also be the total number of variables. In dataset fab2 the methods should detect all 21 truly involved variables. Some more might be found to approximate other non-linearities present in the ground truth.

selection for dataset fab1 still works perfectly. The mean computation time was even reduced a bit. This is because of the distribution of the BIC loops there are fewer model fits needed in total. For dataset fab2 the selection of the true variables improved. Only in one of ten runs a variable was removed despite belonging to the ground truth. Furthermore, a deeper analysis of the final model shows the possibility of an interpretation which we described in section 5.6 as a desirable property.

6.6.1. Interpretation of the Final Model

Let us consider the variables from one of the ten runs. There were a total of 27 selected variables. The final differences d in the BIC values are illustrated in Figure 6.3. Note the logarithmic y-scale. Without knowing anything about the ground truth analyzing this final values can bring some important insight. The absolute values of the d_j have no significance since they depend on the sample size n. However, the relative difference in the values allow for some interpretation. The first observation is that the covariates x_1 to x_{15} are in the same range. An exclusion to this is x_{11} which has a larger value than the others. This might be an indication that it is present in another non-linearity that is not part of the scope of the model. This could be a three-fold interaction or an interaction with a square of a variable. This considerations could lead to testing those combinations and ending up finding $x_5^2 x_{11}$.

Let us now consider the values of the two-fold interactions. Their values are also in the same range, which could lead to the conclusion that there is nothing more going on. The comparison of the squares show that there seems to be two groups. We have x_8^2, x_9^2, x_{13}^2 with values d barely smaller than zero. By contrast there are x_1^2, x_5^2, x_{10}^2 with very large values and x_{11}^2 with an intermediate value. Since x_{11}^2 lies in the range of the covariates and the two-fold interactions one could conclude that this variable is simply part of the ground truth itself. The three squares with values slightly smaller than zero might be part of some more complicated non-linearities or indicate that the corresponding covariate is part of such. One can at least conclude that they play a greater role in the ground truth than the other covariates selected. Checking the ground truth shows that all three appear twice in some three-fold and four-fold interactions. The squares with the largest values indicate that their role is more important and possible interactions could be investigated. This might lead to finding $x_1^2 x_{10}^2$ and $x_5^2 x_{11}$.

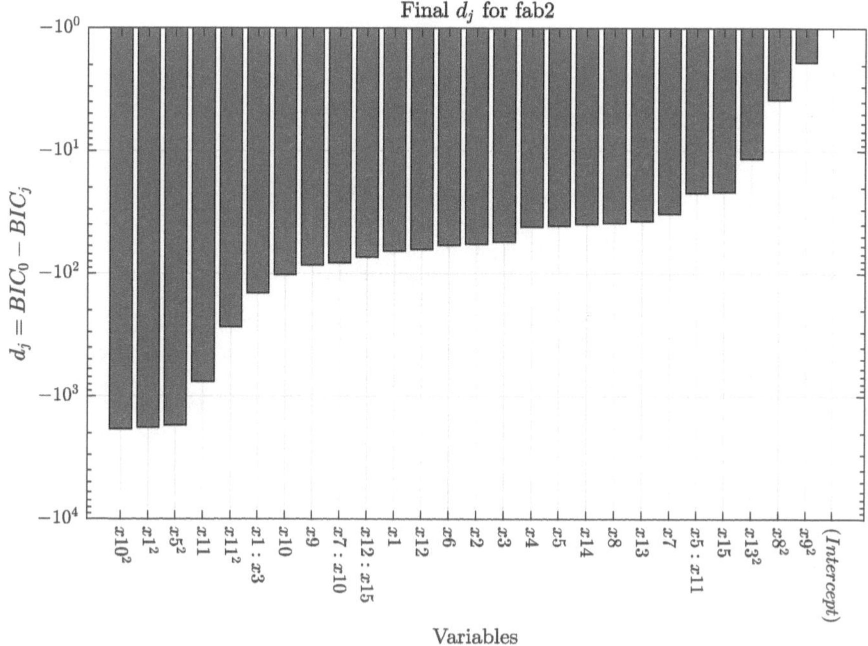

Fig. 6.3.: Differences in BIC values after final model is selected.

This example shows that the greedy selection of variables allows for some interpretation and the researcher could find some more relationships of variables in using this model as a starting point and test some other non-linearities himself.

7. Results on Real World Data

The model selection procedure is conducted ten times on each dataset. This is performed for *stepwiseglm* sampled, WBIC and the neural network. In *stepwiseglm* and WBIC different models might be selected due to the sampling. For the neural network different results occur due to the random initialization of the network weights. The number of hidden neurons for the neural network was set to twice the number of parameters in the dataset. Determining the optimal number of hidden neurons is rather difficult, and we use the same setting as experts in the field of prospectivity modeling recommended. The activation function is the logistic function. Out of the ten runs the model that gives the best F_1 score on the training data is used for testing the performance on the test data. The methods are compared mainly in terms of area under the precision-recall curve (AUPR) and the F_1-score. We further give the TPR and PREC for every method using a threshold of 0.5.

We use bootstrapping to test the methods. From the test set we created 1000 new test sets through drawing with replacement and evaluated the performance of the corresponding methods. The two versions of *stepwiseglm*, our proposed method WBIC and a neural network are compared with each other. The neural network is supposed to serve as a reference for the classification performance of the selected models. In regards of the different model selection method particular emphasis is put on the following criteria:

- Mean number of variables selected for the final model,

- total number of different selected variables over 10 runs,

- number of variables selected every run,

- model selection time.

In general, having a similar performance of different models, the model with fewer variables is to be preferred. So a key point in analyzing the different model selection approaches is the number of selected variables. Furthermore, for *stepwiseglm* sampled and WBIC it is also interesting to see the difference in the models over different runs. Since both methods depend on the sample that is taken from the full training data it is important to see how much the model varies over these different samples. The values are displayed as the mean $\pm$ the standard deviation of 10 runs. The computation time is rounded to full seconds. For *stepwiseglm* full there is no deviation since it needs to be run only once on the training data. The number of variables displayed for the neural networks is the total number of weights of the network.

7.1. Ds1.10

The first dataset we analyze is ds1.10. Here the training data consisted of 21 573 examples, 617 of which are positive. Thus the sample used for training consists of 1851 examples where the fraction of positive events is 0.33. The results of the model selection process are displayed in Table 7.1.

Our proposed method WBIC is almost a magnitude faster than *stepwiseglm* sampled. Even for ten runs the computation time is five times faster than for *stepwiseglm* full. The resulting models of WBIC contain only about half the number of variables of the *stepwiseglm* methods.

	Runtime (s)	# variables	Different Variables	Common Variables
WBIC	7 ± 0	14.3 ± 0.7	19	10
stepwiseglm sampled	52 ± 26	26.3 ± 5.1	51	9
stepwiseglm full	354	30	-	-
Neural Network H20	24 ± 20	241	-	-

Tab. 7.1.: Summary of the model selection process for ds1.10.

Furthermore, there appear only 19 different variables over all ten runs of which 10 appear in every model. Contrary, for the *stepwiseglm* sampled method there are over 50 variables in total but only 9 appear in ever model. With a mean of 14 variables in every model this means about 70% of the variables in every model appear every time. Contrary, for *stepwiseglm* sampled this is only 35%, its models differ largely. The neural network with 20 hidden neurons is the second fastest method. Considering the weights as variables the final neural network model has 241 variables. With regards to the model selection process our method seems preferable to the *stepwiseglm* methods. However, it is crucial that the selected model does also perform well on the classification task of unseen data. The models used for classification are the ones with the largest F_1-score on the full training data. The results for the area under the precision-recall curve, the true positive rate, the true negative rate, the precision as well as the F_1-score are given in Table 7.2. Furthermore, Table 7.3 shows the confusion matrices for the predictions using a cutoff value 0.5, i.e. all scores below 0.5 are set to zero and all scores greater equal to 0.5 are set to one.

	AUPR	TPR	TNR	PREC	F_1-score
WBIC	0.5322	0.3102	0.9996	0.9667	0.4696
stepwiseglm sampled	0.4819	0.7433	0.9027	0.2169	0.3358
stepwiseglm full	0.5392	0.3262	0.9996	0.9683	0.4880
Neural Network H20	0.5775	0.3583	0.9986	0.9054	0.5134

Tab. 7.2.: Summary of of prediction ability of the different methods on ds1.10

<table>
<tr><th colspan="3">WBIC
Predicted</th><th colspan="3">*stepwiseglm* samp
Predicted</th><th colspan="3">*stepwiseglm* full
Predicted</th><th colspan="3">Neural Net H20
Predicted</th></tr>
<tr><td></td><td>0</td><td>1</td><td></td><td>0</td><td>1</td><td></td><td>0</td><td>1</td><td></td><td>0</td><td>1</td></tr>
<tr><td>Actual 0</td><td>5158</td><td>2</td><td>Actual 0</td><td>4658</td><td>502</td><td>Actual 0</td><td>5158</td><td>2</td><td>Actual 0</td><td>5153</td><td>7</td></tr>
<tr><td>1</td><td>129</td><td>58</td><td>1</td><td>48</td><td>139</td><td>1</td><td>126</td><td>61</td><td>1</td><td>120</td><td>67</td></tr>
</table>

Tab. 7.3.: Confusion matrices for ds1.10 using 0.5 as cutoff.

Analyzing the area under the precision-recall curve (AUPR) we can see that the neural network outperforms the other methods. But that was to be expected. However, WBIC has a higher precision which is very important in prospectivity modeling. The *stepwiseglm* sampled performs worse than the other methods. One reason is that it was trained on a nearly balanced sample ($\bar{y} = 0.33$) but the predictions are made on the dataset with rare events. This results in an overestimation of the positive event which in turn gives a much larger true positive rate but also a much smaller precision. For a fair comparison a correction on the parameter estimates would need to be applied. But this could not be applied since there is no possibility to change the parameter estimates in the resulting model of the MATLAB function *stepwiseglm*. Nevertheless, even a bias correction as described in section 4.6.2 would only shift the linear hyperplane which would not lead to a change in the order of the scores. Hence the AUPR would still be the same. Our proposed method WBIC performs nearly identical to the *stepwiseglm* full with minimal advantages for the latter. The confusion matrices show that *stepwiseglm* full was able to find three more positive cases while having identical values otherwise. The corresponding precision-recall curves are shown in Figure 7.1.

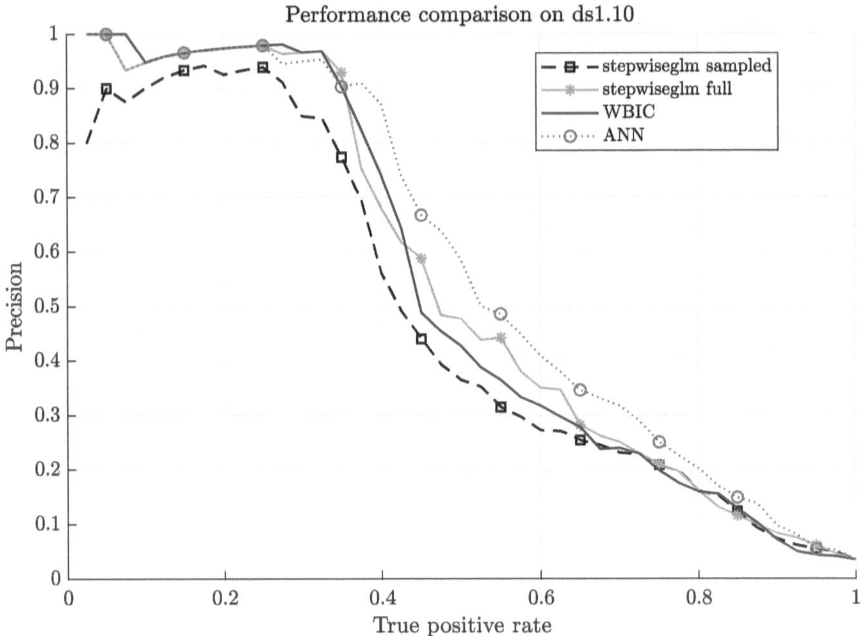

Fig. 7.1.: Precision-recall curve for dataset ds1.10.

To summarize, our proposed method selects a model that performs nearly as good as the *stepwiseglm* full. Especially until reaching a true positive rate of 0.45 the two methods are basically identical. Even the neural network did not perform better in this respect. Our method reaches this performance needing only a fraction of the time for the model selection. Furthermore the final model had only half as many variables as *stepwiseglm* full. Considering the almost identical performance leads to the conclusion that WBIC was able to detect more important variables and combinations of those.

7.2. Ds1.100

We continue with the enlargement of the ds1.10 dataset. Instead of using only the top ten variables of the principal component analysis of the ds1 dataset we now consider the top

100 variables. This results in over 5000 variables that are considered for the inclusion in the model. A summary of the model selection process is given in Table 7.4.

	Runtime (s)	# variables	Different Variables	Common Vars
WBIC	$1\,475 \pm 315$	14.6 ± 1.7	40	6
stepwiseglm sampled	$10\,133 \pm 5\,410$	94.3 ± 17.4	348	12
stepwiseglm full	$97\,777$	112	-	-
Neural Network H200	27 ± 8	$20\,401$	-	-

Tab. 7.4.: Summary of the model selection process for ds1.100.

Despite the large number of weights the neural network was by far the fastest method. Our proposed method outperformed the *stepwiseglm* full and sampled method regarding the time needed. Running ten model selections with WBIC is still over five times faster than one run of *stepwiseglm* full. Astonishing is the small number of variables selected for the final model in our WBIC. Only around 15 of initial over 5000 variables are selected. Thereof six variables are selected in every model, that is about 40%. The sampled version of *stepwiseglm* selects around 95 variables for the final model of which only 12 appear in every model, only 13%. In ten runs there are a total of 348 different variables selected. This means the selected model differs largely for every run as it did with the ds1.10 dataset. The *stepwiseglm* full selected almost 100 variables more than WBIC. Using again the models with the largest F_1-score on the training data for classification we obtain the results displayed in Table 7.5. The confusion matrices corresponding to a cutoff value of 0.5 are shown in Table 7.6.

	AUPR	TPR	TNR	PREC	F_1-score
WBIC	0.6418	0.4652	0.9979	0.8878	0.6105
stepwiseglm sampled	0.6317	0.8182	0.9058	0.2382	0.3685
stepwiseglm full	0.7041	0.5294	0.9971	0.8684	0.6578
Neural Network H200	0.6819	0.4866	0.9983	0.9100	0.6341

Tab. 7.5.: Summary of of prediction ability of the different methods on ds1.100.

WBIC

		Predicted 0	Predicted 1
Actual	0	5149	11
	1	100	87

***stepwiseglm* samp**

		Predicted 0	Predicted 1
Actual	0	4674	486
	1	35	152

***stepwiseglm* full**

		Predicted 0	Predicted 1
Actual	0	5145	15
	1	88	99

Neural Net H200

		Predicted 0	Predicted 1
Actual	0	5151	9
	1	96	91

Tab. 7.6.: Confusion matrices for ds1.100 using 0.5 as cutoff.

The first observation we can make is that all methods should perform better than on the ds1.10 dataset since the ten variables used there are also part of this dataset. This is indeed the case. Surprisingly, the *stepwiseglm* full seems to be the best model. It even outperforms the neural network in AUPR. Our WBIC method has a smaller AUPR value and detects

12 true positive examples less than *stepwiseglm* full. However, checking Figure 7.2 we see that WBIC, *stepwiseglm* and the neural network exhibit the same performance until a true positive rate of 0.25. Then the performance of WBIC drops a bit until we have again an equal performance at a true positive rate of 0.5. But this is far better then one would expect with 100 variables less in the model. Even better, the first 37 examples with the largest scores in WBIC are all actual positive. This can be seen in Figure 7.2 as WBIC still has a precision of 1 at the true positive rate of 0.2.

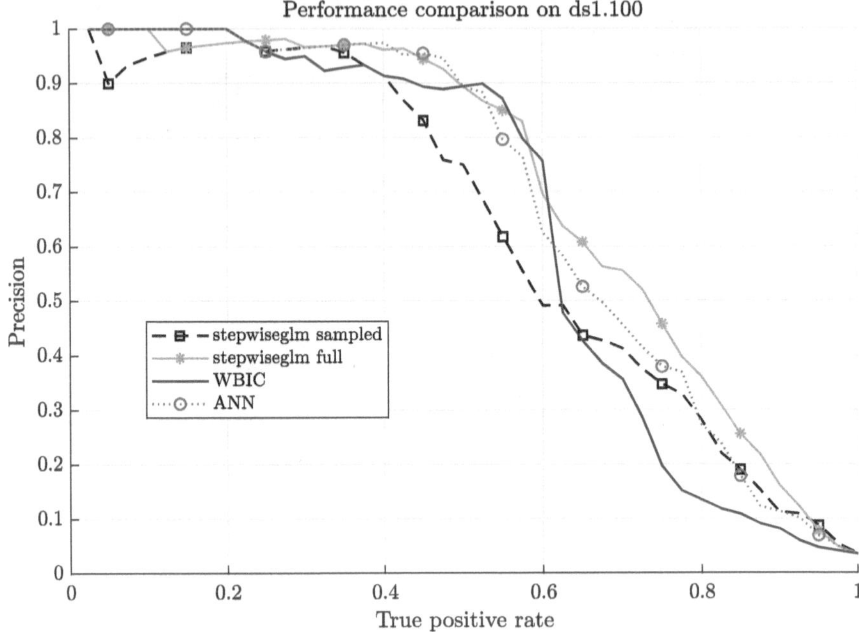

Fig. 7.2.: Precision-recall curve for dataset ds1.100.

Comparing the time needed for the model selection and the fact that WBIC selected approximately 100 fewer variables than *stepwiseglm* full while still having a classification performance that is not much worse we can conclude that our method is able to detect important variables and non-linearities that contribute for classification and therefore partly explain the underlying truth.

7.3. Covtype

Now we come to the covtype dataset. The original dataset has 55 variables, but as mentioned in section 5.3.2 we discarded the 44 binary features. Thus there are only 10 real valued variables considered for training. The model selection process is summarized in Table 7.7.

The neural network is again the fastest. Our method WBIC is faster than *stepwiseglm* sampled and ten runs are still twice as fast as *stepwiseglm* full in total. The number of selected variables is relatively stable around 35 for every model. Furthermore, 22 variables are selected in every model, i.e. approximately 63% of the model is the same in every run. A similar result is obtained for *stepwiseglm* sample where we have around 47 variables in a model of which

	Runtime (s)	# variables	Different Variables	Common Vars
WBIC	$1\,533 \pm 303$	34.4 ± 2.7	51	22
stepwiseglm sampled	$4\,197 \pm 956$	47.3 ± 3.2	61	30
stepwiseglm full	$29\,028$	59	-	-
Neural Network H20	743 ± 276	241	-	-

Tab. 7.7.: Summary of the model selection process for Covtype.

approximately 64% is the same in every run. Table 7.8 summarizes the classification results on the test set. Table 7.9 shows the confusion matrices using again a cutoff value of 0.5.

	AUPR	TPR	TNR	PREC	F_1-score
WBIC	0.7100	0.6464	0.9813	0.6908	0.6679
stepwiseglm sampled	0.6833	0.9463	0.9414	0.5098	0.6627
stepwiseglm full	0.7165	0.6518	0.9814	0.6936	0.6721
Neural Network H20	0.8285	0.7351	0.9848	0.7577	0.7462

Tab. 7.8.: Summary of of prediction ability of the different methods on Covtype.

WBIC			*stepwiseglm* **samp**			*stepwiseglm* **full**			**Neural Net H20**		
	Predicted			Predicted			Predicted			Predicted	
	0	1		0	1		0	1		0	1
Actual 0	107129	2036	Actual 0	102763	6402	Actual 0	107139	2046	Actual 0	107511	1654
Actual 1	2488	4549	Actual 1	378	6659	Actual 1	2450	4587	Actual 1	1864	5173

Tab. 7.9.: Confusion matrices for Covtype using 0.5 as cutoff.

On Covtype the neural network outperforms the other methods by far. The AUPR score is more than 0.1 larger than the ones of WBIC and *stepwiseglm* full. WBIC and *stepwiseglm* full again exhibit a similar performance. Figure 7.3 shows that the small difference lies in the first few predictionss. From a true positive value of 0.15 both methods seem to be equal in their predictions. Contrary to ds1.10 and ds1.100, the neural network exhibits a far better performance. This opens up the possibility to enhance predictions of WBIC through including more non-linearities. This is possible because of the small number of variables. We add all variables of a cubic model to our training matrix. This results in a model selection time that was about ten times longer than WBIC with a quadratic model. However, this would still be twice as fast as *stepwiseglm* full. Figure 7.4 shows the updated precision recall curve. WBIC now refers to our method with a starting cubic model. It can be seen that the performance improved significantly, and it comes close to the neural network performance. It has a AUPR value of 0.78. However, the final model consisted of 72 variables, which makes it inappropriate or at least more difficult to interpret. But it surely shows the ability of the model selection to improve predictions with more non-linearities without over-fitting on the training data.

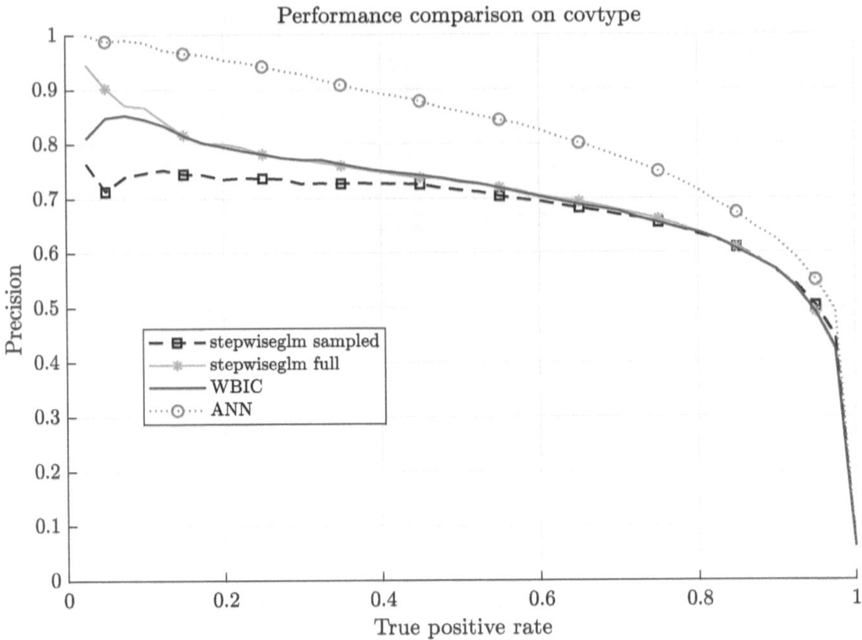

Fig. 7.3.: Precision-recall curve for dataset Covtype.

7.4. Cod-RNA

The Cod-RNA dataset only consists of eight predictor variables. This results in a small number of possible variables. Hence the model selection process does not take much time. The results of the model selection are summarized in Table 7.10.

	Runtime (s)	# variables	Different Variables	Common Vars
WBIC	60 ± 18	16.4 ± 3.1	27	9
stepwiseglm sampled	376 ± 123	26.9 ± 3.3	44	15
stepwiseglm full	$4\,044$	41	-	-
Neural Network H16	97 ± 25	161	-	-

Tab. 7.10.: Summary of the model selection process on Cod-RNA.

Our WBIC only needs about one minute for one selection run. This is a bit faster than the neural network and over five times faster than *stepwiseglm* sampled. The *stepwiseglm* full even takes over an hour for the selection. WBIC selects around 16 variables of which 56% are present in every model. The sampled version of *stepwiseglm* selects over ten more variables on average. The percentage of variables that appear in every model is also 56%. The full version selects two and a half times more variables than WBIC. Examining the performance on the test set we can see that all methods exhibit similar AUPR values, see Table7.11.

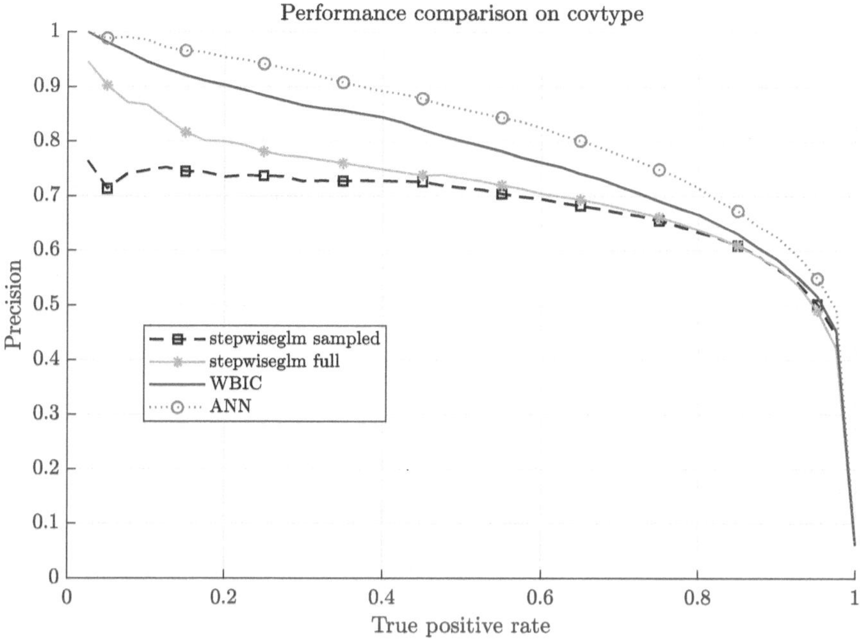

Fig. 7.4.: Precision-recall curve for dataset Covtype. WBIC started with a cubic model.

	AUPR	TPR	TNR	PREC	F_1-score
WBIC	0.8349	0.7380	0.9914	0.8214	0.7775
stepwiseglm sampled	0.8345	0.9512	0.9687	0.6208	0.7513
stepwiseglm full	0.8470	0.7518	0.9914	0.8241	0.7863
Neural Network H16	0.8558	0.7841	0.9899	0.8063	0.7951

Tab. 7.11.: Summary of of prediction ability of the different methods on Cod-RNA.

The *stepwiseglm* sampled version again overestimates the positive event resulting in a much larger true positive rate and a much smaller precision than the other methods. However, regarding the F_1-score it performs almost as good as the other methods. Figure 7.5 shows that all methods are quite close to each other. The neural network has a larger precision for the largest scores but is approaching the other methods with increasing true positive rate.

WBIC	Predicted 0	Predicted 1		***stepwiseglm* samp**	Predicted 0	Predicted 1		***stepwiseglm* full**	Predicted 0	Predicted 1		**Neural Net H16**	Predicted 0	Predicted 1
Actual 0	41 538	362		Actual 0	40 589	1 311		Actual 0	41 538	362		Actual 0	41 475	425
Actual 1	591	1 665		Actual 1	110	2 146		Actual 1	560	1 696		Actual 1	487	1 769

Tab. 7.12.: Confusion matrices for Cod-RNA using 0.5 as cutoff.

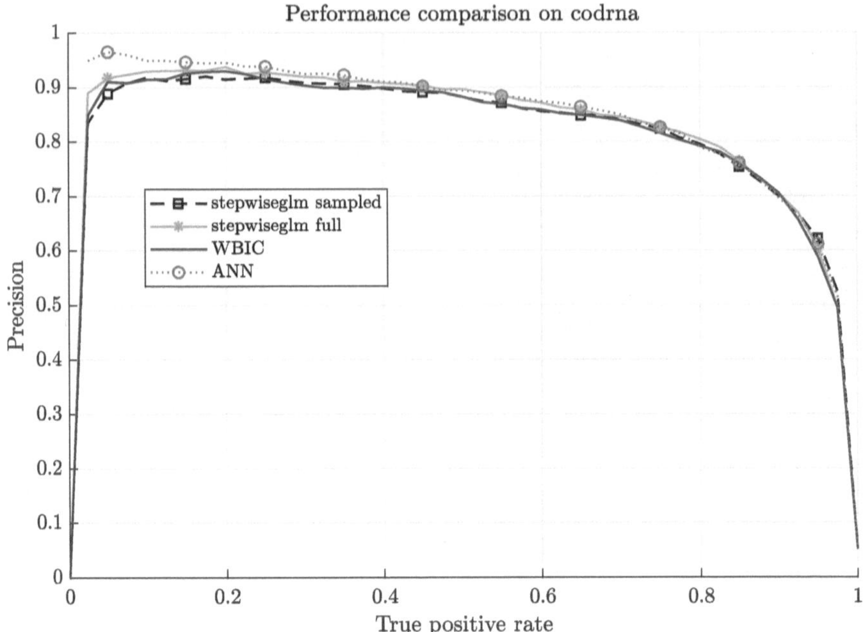

Fig. 7.5.: Precision-recall curve for dataset Cod-RNA.

Again, WBIC is faster and selects fewer variables while exhibiting the same classification performance as the *stepwiseglm* versions.

7.5. Ghana Gold Mineralisation Prospection

In this section we investigate the performance of our suggested model selection on the exploration of gold mineralisations in Ghana. This is the kind of data our method was developed for. Before the model selection is conducted the corresponding data is described in more detail.

7.5.1. Model Area and Variable Description

The information about the data are taken from [6] where the author conducted a classification on that area. A neural network and logistic regression are compared. Here the input variables to the neural network were chosen carefully through a study. The same is the case for logistic regression. An analysis was conducted deciding which variables and possible twofold interactions to include in the LR model. This was done by hand and this is where our method could support the researcher.

The model area is located in the south-western part of Ghana, see Figure 7.6. It covers a total area of approximately $60\,100$ km^2. A total of 30 predictor variables are created from collected data from the region using geology, tectonic and geophysics. For instance, Figure 7.7 shows the four variables describing magnetic characteristics. All variables are scaled to range between zero and one, binary variables excluded. There are a total of $7\,361$ positive datapoints describing gold mineralisations. This is only about 0.14% of all datapoints. They are located

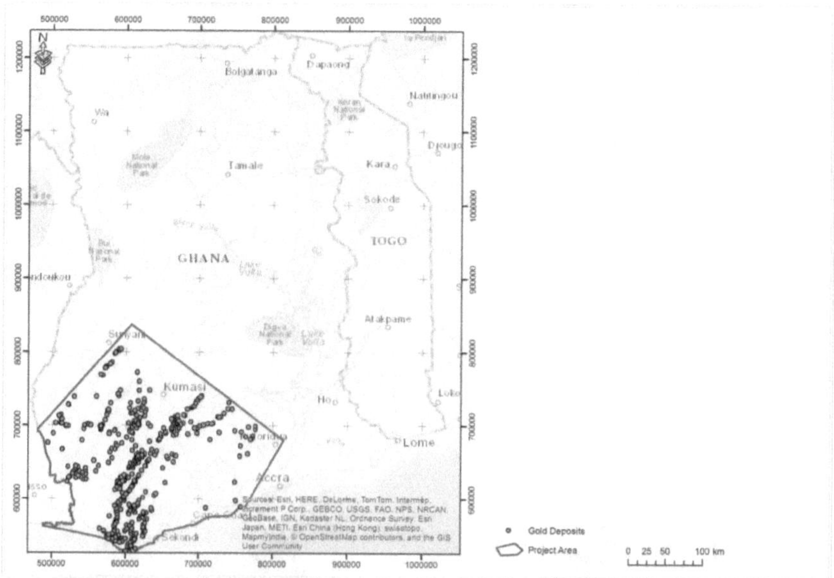

Fig. 7.6.: Model area in the south-western part of Ghana. Picture provided by Beak Consultants GmbH.

as shown in Figure 7.8. Gold mineralisations can emerge through different processes. In [6], the author classifies the mineralisations into four different types. Hence, there might not be a best model for all mineralisations but only for a special type whereas another type might need a different model for classification. This complicates the model selection since we do not distinguish between gold mineralisations. The training area is a rectangle area in the north of the model region. It is shown in Figure 7.9. It contains nearly three million datapoints of which only 4174 are positive.

7.5.2. Neural Network Performance

We will start with the result of different variations of neural networks. This is done to obtain a reference for possible performances and will help to put the result of the model selection in a context. We train four different neural networks using

i) the full training area,

ii) preselected datapoints in the training area,

iii) preselected datapoints with preselected variables,

iv) preselected datapoints with preselected variables and replicate positive datapoints to get a balanced sample.

Using the full training area with all variables is how many people imagine neural networks to work like. However this is not always the best practice. The preselected datapoints are chosen in [6] in collaboration with experts from the company Beak Consultants GmbH from Freiberg, Saxony, Germany. The preselected variables were carefully chosen using some expert

Fig. 7.7.: Rocks of the earth crust possess different magnetization. Using aeromagnetic measurements one can determine structures of the earth crust. The four figures show the magnetic alignment in south-north and west-east direction as well as the slope gradient and the scaled absolute value.

knowledge and trial-and-error. Adding copies of positive datapoints to create a balanced sample will help neural network to give predictions greater than 0.5. Figure 7.10 shows the predictions of the trained neural networks for the four cases. For case i) we see a few spots with large predictions. The rest of the model area is basically predicted with zero potential. Case ii) has even fewer spots with large predictions. In case iii) one cannot see anything different but zero. This is because the maximum value of the predictions is only about 0.09. Case iv) finally shows some structure. There seems to be some streams of very large potential close to one. A comparison with the true mineralisations and the final WBIC model is shown later. The network correctly predicts the area in the south-east with no mineralisations with a small potential. Also a lot of areas of mineralisations have been assigned large potentials.

From the visual point of view one could conclude that the neural network of case iv) does a decent job. It provides some rough intuition about the areas the mineralisations are located. However, if we only consider the sheer statistical evaluation the first network would be the preferred one. This is indicated in Table 7.13 and Table 7.14 which show the confusion

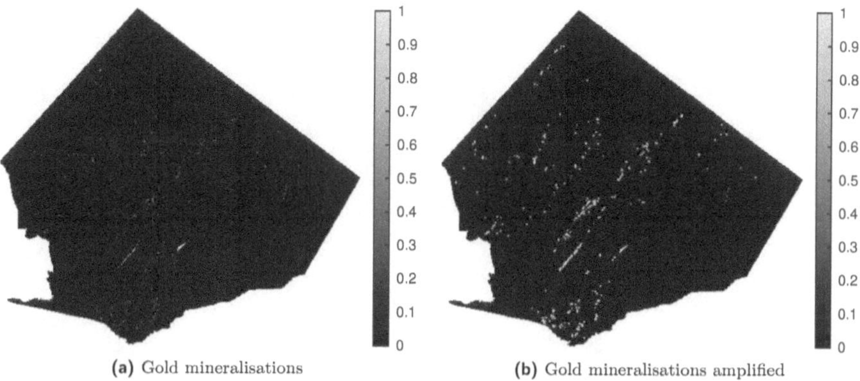

Fig. 7.8.: Location of known gold mineralisations in the model area (a) in original size and (b) enlarged for better visualization.

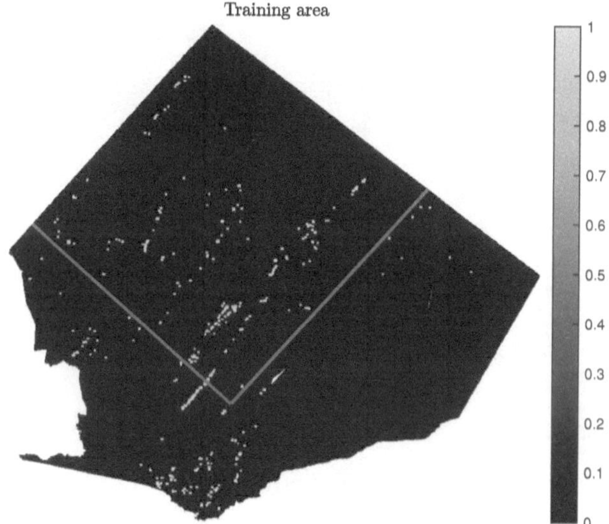

Fig. 7.9.: The red line confines the training area. Everything outside is used for testing purposes.

matrices for the complete model area (including the training area) and the test area of the model region, respectively.

7.5.3. BWIC: Preliminary Considerations

As the results of the neural network in the previous subsection shows one may not expect that the model selection will do an outstanding job in classification. The goal should be to create a model that is able to make classifications that come close to those of the neural network trained on case iv). Another point to consider is the extreme rarity of the target event. Using the sampling scheme as we did on the other datasets we would collect a total of 8 000 negative examples and perform a model selection on those and the almost 4 000 positive

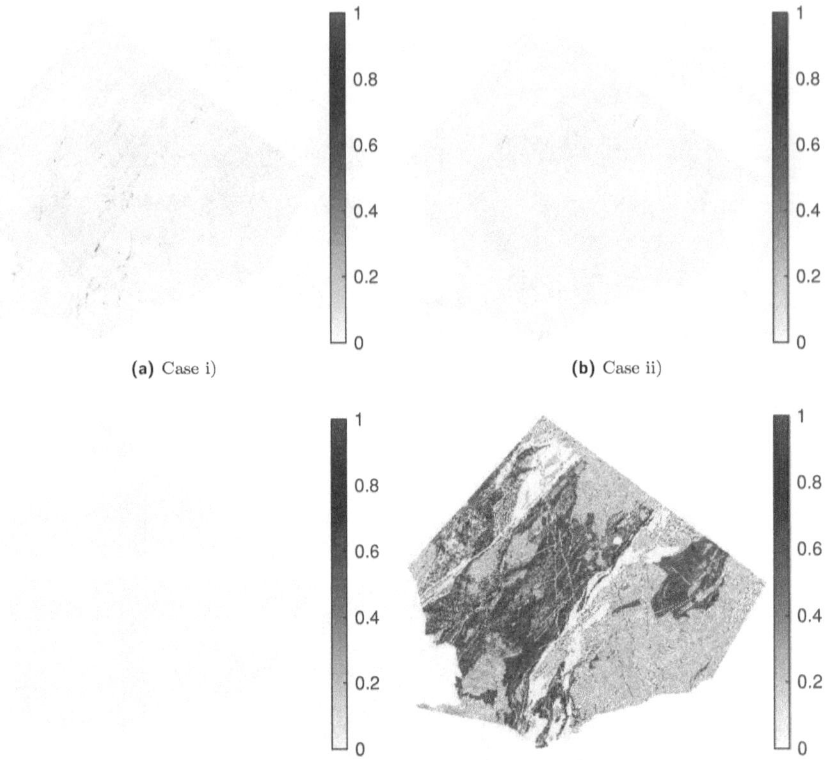

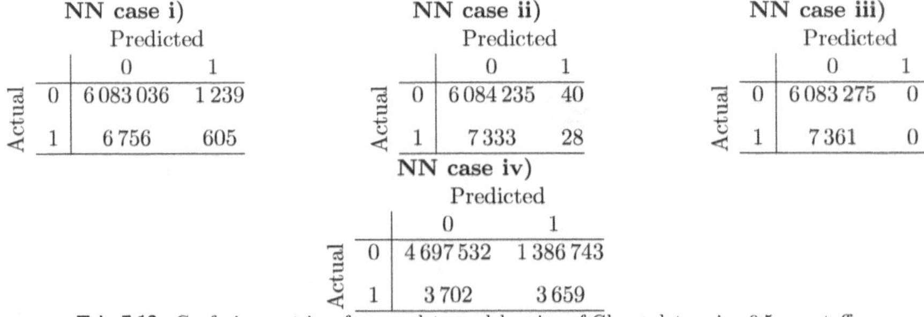

(a) Case i)   (b) Case ii)

(c) Case iii)   (d) Case iv)

Fig. 7.10.: Predictions of the neural networks for cases i) to iv).

NN case i)

		Predicted	
		0	1
Actual	0	6 083 036	1 239
	1	6 756	605

NN case ii)

		Predicted	
		0	1
Actual	0	6 084 235	40
	1	7 333	28

NN case iii)

		Predicted	
		0	1
Actual	0	6 083 275	0
	1	7 361	0

NN case iv)

		Predicted	
		0	1
Actual	0	4 697 532	1 386 743
	1	3 702	3 659

Tab. 7.13.: Confusion matrices for complete model region of Ghana data using 0.5 as cutoff.

examples. This makes the model largely dependent on the 8 000 randomly collected negative examples since possible important variables might not be collected because of the lack of negative datapoints that could make this variable necessary.

We use three different settings for the model selection and compare them to each other.

| | NN case i) | | | NN case ii) | | | NN case iii) | | | NN case iv) | |
| | Predicted | | | Predicted | | | Predicted | | | Predicted | |
	0	1		0	1		0	1		0	1
Actual 0	3 104 430	810	Actual 0	3 106 163	0	Actual 0	3 106 163	0	Actual 0	2 481 844	624 319
Actual 1	3	71	Actual 1	3 187	0	Actual 1	3 187	0	Actual 1	1 914	1 273

Tab. 7.14.: Confusion matrices for test area of Ghana data using 0.5 as cutoff.

The identification of variables that appear in every approach will also be an interesting point we are going to consider. The first approach is simply taking the training area and run the model selection ten times as we did on the other datasets. We then select the model with the best performance on the training area as final model for comparison on the test set.

In the second approach we artificially increase the occurrence of the target. This is done by assigning a positive target to negative examples in a neighborhood of a real positive example. This applies the same idea as seen in Figure 7.8(b) where we amplified the targets for better visualization. This is now done in the same manner for the dataset we use for the model selection. This will give more positive targets and therefore also more collected negative samples. In addition, this introduces some spatial dependency. We will take up this thought later on. We perform the model selection for different sizes of the neighborhood.

As third approach we perform a preselection of negative datapoints from which we can create the random sample. Considering the 30 dimensional space of all predictor variables. There are most likely a lot of negative datapoints that have no positive example in their neighborhood due to the occurrence of the target of only 0.1%. Hence the preselection should select negative datapoints that are close to positive examples in the given variable space. These are the one we need a good decision boundary for in order to separate them from the positive examples. To determine such negative examples we use a self-organizing-map. After the introduction of self-organizing-maps in the next subsection we present the results of the three approaches.

7.5.4. Self-Organizing-Maps (SOM)

Self-organizing-maps are a type of an artificial neural network. They belong to the group of unsupervised learning. They were first introduced by Kohonen in 1982 [35]. A SOM clusters data in a high dimensional space and projects it onto a two dimensional space. It can also project it to another subspace of the initial input space, but since the two dimensional case is the most common we will describe this one. It consists of a user-defined number of weight vectors that are used for the clustering of the input. These weights are either initialized randomly or are evenly distributed in the two dimensional space spanned by the two largest principal component eigenvectors. Then for every example its Euclidean distance to every weight vector is calculated. The weight vector which is the closest to the input will be moved in the direction of the input. Weight vectors that are further away will also be moved in direction of this input, but the value of movement decreases with the distance so the majority of weight vectors is not moved. This is executed over a large sample of inputs. At the end, the final location of the weight vectors define a center of a cluster and every new input is assigned to the cluster of the nearest weight vector. Spatial awareness is becoming more and more important [58] and maybe SOM can contribute as an alternative.

We build a SOM of our training area. We then consider only the negative datapoints that are located in a cluster that contains also some positive datapoints. The negative datapoints in clusters with no positive examples will most likely have little to no effect on the model selection. We build a SOM with 256 clusters, spanning a two dimensional field of 16 times 16 weight vectors. This SOM is trained with all datapoints from the training area. Interesting is the distribution of the positive datapoints over the cluster. This is displayed in Figure 7.11. A lot of clusters do not contain a single positive example. Hence the negative examples in

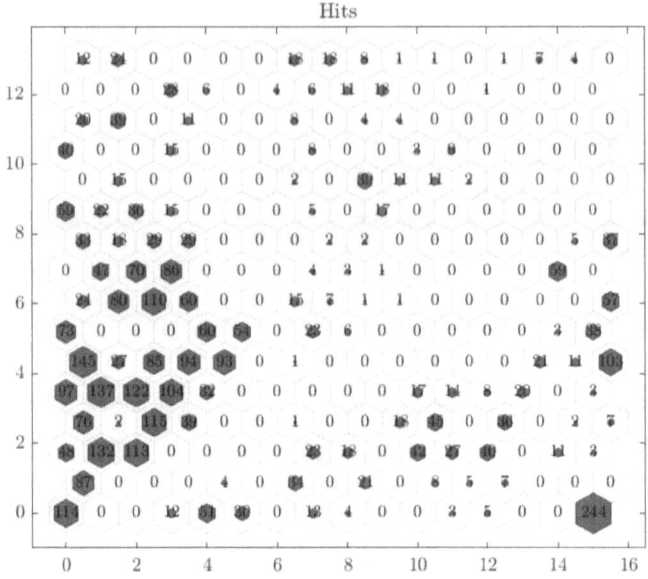

Fig. 7.11.: Number of positive datapoints that are contained in each bin of the SOM. Mineralisations in the same bin exhibit a similar structure in their corresponding features.

those clusters will not be considered for the sampling process. We then use different values for the number of positive events a cluster should contain in order to be included in the training data.

7.5.5. WBIC Model Selection Results

Running the model selection using the complete training area is the same as using $k = 1$ in the approach for enlarging the positive target and is summarized together with the other values in Table 7.15. The fraction of positive events in the training area increases. The runtime of the model selection does not differ too much. The number of variables each version selects increases with the increase of k. So does the number of different variables. However, the number of variables that are selected in every method do not increase much. Enlarging the positive target assigns positive values to the datapoints next to a target. This induces some sort of spatial dependency since a distance to some geological entity can become important. This in turn will select the variable corresponding to that entity for the model. Although there will be no mineralisation on that point some structures can be revealed. This can be seen in Figure 7.12. Next, we evaluate the model selection process for the third approach using the preselection of negative datapoints with the trained SOM. The results are given in Table 7.16. Here, the rarity is more or less the same for every version. The runtime decreases because the size of the sample does also decrease. With the exception of $c = 80$ the number of variables in the models and the number of overall selected variables are almost identical.

# pos	Rarity (%)	Runtime (s)	# variables	Different Variables	Common Vars
k=1	0.14	$1\,743 \pm 54$	19.5 ± 2.2	33	10
k=2	0.21	$1\,833 \pm 80$	24.1 ± 2.0	49	9
k=4	0.37	$1\,862 \pm 50$	35.1 ± 3.0	70	13
k=6	0.58	$2\,125 \pm 120$	38.9 ± 2.4	77	15
k=8	0.82	$2\,222 \pm 148$	43.6 ± 3.2	91	13
k=10	1.1	$2\,094 \pm 123$	49.5 ± 4.8	104	12

Tab. 7.15.: Summary of the model selection process using different sizes k of neighboring points of positive targets that have also been assigned positive.

Threshold c	Rarity (%)	Runtime (s)	# variables	Different Variables	Common Vars
c=5	0.24	$1\,242 \pm 50$	17.8 ± 1.1	27	12
c=10	0.26	$1\,163 \pm 34$	17.6 ± 3.1	32	9
c=20	0.32	903 ± 39	13.6 ± 1.9	32	5
c=40	0.36	493 ± 15	16.7 ± 2.1	30	8
c=80	0.35	240 ± 16	10.6 ± 1.6	20	5

Tab. 7.16.: Summary of the model selection process using different sizes c of minimum number of positive targets a cluster has to contain in order to consider the negative points within this cluster.

For every approach we chose the best model as the one that has the best performance for the original training region in the AUPR score. The summary of the performance of these models on the test set is shown in Table 7.17. While the AUPR scores for the training area range from 0.0366 to 0.0602 they do not differ that much for the test area. For the test set the model trained on the original training area seems to generalize best. But the overall values are as bad as they were for neural networks.

However, the interesting part really is the visualization of the prediction results. Figure 7.12 shows the change in prediction with the increase of the value k. We can see that there are structures evolving as the value of k increases. With larger values of k, i.e. extending the positive target to neighboring points, there are more and more lines emerging in the prediction. Figure 7.13 shows the predictions of the model with $k = 10$ and the known gold mineralisations. One can clearly see that a lot of gold mineralisations lie on or next to such a line of larger predictions. Although this will in some sort worsen the prediction statistics since there are still plenty of datapoints on the lines that do not cover a mineralisations the model can still be a great guidance and offer insight.

Finally, let us analyze the selected variables and try to draw some conclusion from it. Table 7.18 shows the variables that were selected in 9 out of 10 runs for every value of k. This number of variables increases steadily in contrast to the number of selected variables selected in 10 out of 10 runs that decreased from $k = 6$ to larger k, as can be seen in Table 7.15. A first observation is the importance of the variables $x25$ and $x26$ that show up for every k. These describe the distance to crossings of tectonic faults and tectonic faults that lie in the directions

Approach	AUPR train	AUPR test	# variables
k=1	0.0477	**0.0524**	19
k=2	0.0495	0.0496	28
k=4	0.0488	0.0505	36
k=6	0.0574	0.0450	37
k=8	**0.0602**	0.0383	45
k=10	0.0379	0.0408	55
c=5	0.0436	0.0503	19
c=10	0.0422	0.0463	18
c=20	0.0366	0.0390	13
c=40	0.0367	0.0468	18
c=80	0.0369	0.0475	9

Tab. 7.17.: Summary of the AUPR score for every version on the trianing data and test data, respectively.

$5° - 70°$. They are shown in Figure 7.14. A value of one indicates an overlap with the crossing and zero indicates a distance further afield than a specific value defined by Beak. Closeness to a tectonic fault of this kind seems to be beneficial for the existence of a gold mineralisation since both variables have been assigned a positive parameter estimate. Two interactions that appear for every k are $x1 : x7$ and $x1 : x8$. Variable $x1$ describes the Euclidean distance to type of rock that is not specified in the data. Variables $x7$ and $x8$ describe the euclidean distance to intermediate plutonic rock and mafic volcanic rock, respectively. The overlapping of them with the rock type of variable $x1$ seems also to be beneficial for gold mineralisations indicated again by the positive parameter estimate. They are shown in Figure 7.15. As a last example, consider variable $x11$ which enters the model together with its square only for $k = 8$ and $k = 10$. This variable describes the Euclidean distance to a mainly volcanic sediment rock type. Since they enter the model only for larger k the distance specified beforehand by experts seems not to be large enough. With the enlargement of the positive targets a greater distance is considered and seems to be beneficial for gold mineralisations. The variable is shown together with the mineralisations in Figure 7.16.

Turning now to the approach using the SOM as preselection technique for negative datapoints. Table 7.19 displays the variables that have been selected in 9 out of 10 runs for every threshold c. Figure 7.17 shows the corresponding predictions of the models.

For $c = 5$ one can see some weak structure in the predictions. There are the lines we also see for $k = 2$ for instance. These vanish as the value of c increases but therefor the confidence in predicting the mineralisations in the middle southern part also increases. This is a spot with many mineralisations that are very similar in their features. This is why it is predicted so accurately without almost no false positive by using a threshold of $c = 80$. The variables selected for $c = 80$ are $x25$ and $x26$ with its square that we have already seen in the analysis before. In addition, we have the variables $x1$ and $x3$. Both parameter estimates of these variables are negative indicating that the occurrence of those rocks is not beneficial for gold mineralisations. However, note from the analysis above that the presents of $x1$ together with

k=1	k=2	k=4	k=6	k=8	k=10
Intercept	*Intercept*	*Intercept*	*Intercept*	*Intercept*	*Intercept*
$x1$	$x1$	$x3$	$x3$	$x8$	$x5$
$x3$	$x3$	$x25$	$x25$	$x9$	$x8$
$x4$	$x5$	$x26$	$x26$	$x11$	$x10$
$x5$	$x9$	$x26^2$	$x26^2$	$x17$	$x11$
$x8$	$x25$	$x1:x2$	$x1:x2$	$x25$	$x17$
$x9$	$x26$	$x1:x3$	$x1:x3$	$x26$	$x25$
$x25$	$x26^2$	$x1:x7$	$x1:x7$	$x11^2$	$x26$
$x26$	$x1:x3$	$x1:x8$	$x1:x8$	$x1:x2$	$x11^2$
$x1:x7$	$x1:x7$	$x1:x28$	$x1:x10$	$x1:x3$	$x1:x2$
$x1:x8$	$x1:x8$	$x3:x25$	$x3:x25$	$x1:x7$	$x1:x3$
$x8:x11$	$x3:x25$	$x7:x8$	$x7:x8$	$x1:x8$	$x1:x7$
$x8:x26$	$x12:x26$	$x7:x10$	$x7:x9$	$x1:x10$	$x1:x8$
		$x10:x19$	$x7:x10$	$x1:x28$	$x1:x10$
		$x12:x26$	$x9:x30$	$x3:x25$	$x1:x28$
		$x15:x25$	$x10:x19$	$x7:x8$	$x3:x28$
			$x12:x26$	$x7:x9$	$x4:x9$
			$x15:x25$	$x9:x10$	$x7:x8$
				$x9:x30$	$x7:x10$
				$x12:x26$	$x9:x30$
				$x15:x25$	$x12:x26$
					$x12:x30$
					$x15:x26$

Tab. 7.18.: Variables that were selected 9 out of 10 runs for different values of k.

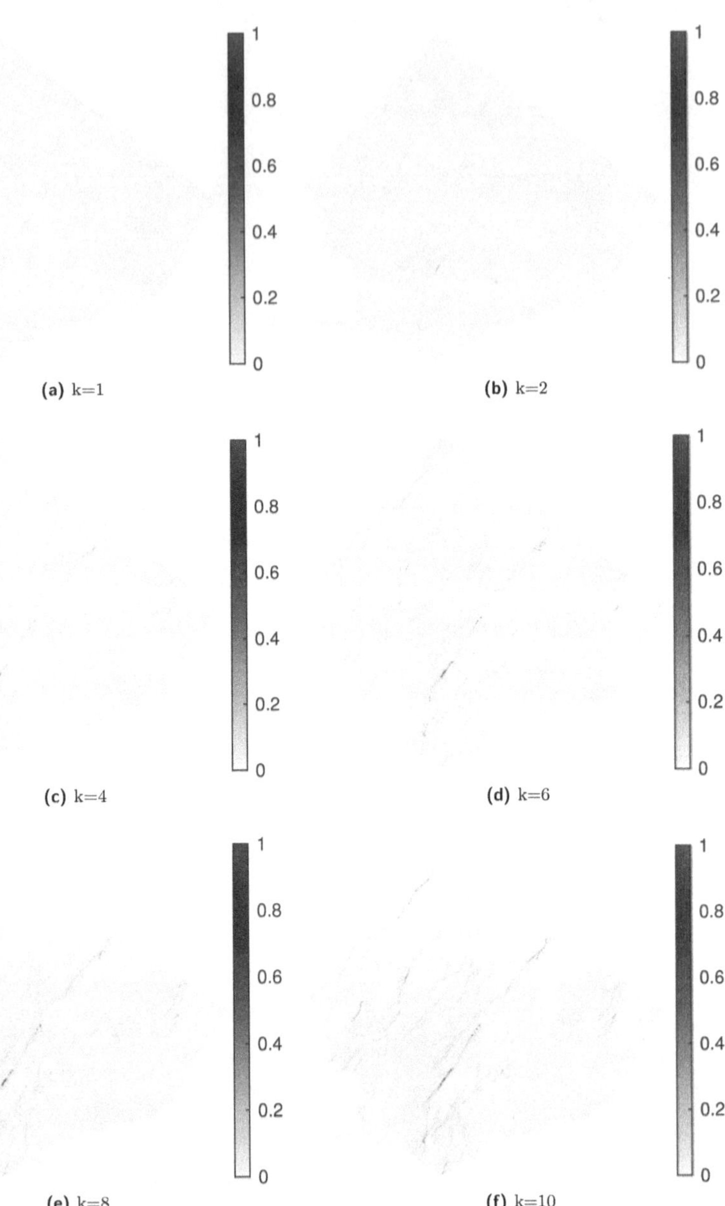

(a) k=1

(b) k=2

(c) k=4

(d) k=6

(e) k=8

(f) k=10

Fig. 7.12.: Model predictions for different models. Every model was trained on the training area using an enlargement k of the positive targets, i.e. the k neighboring values of a positive target have also been assigned to be positive.

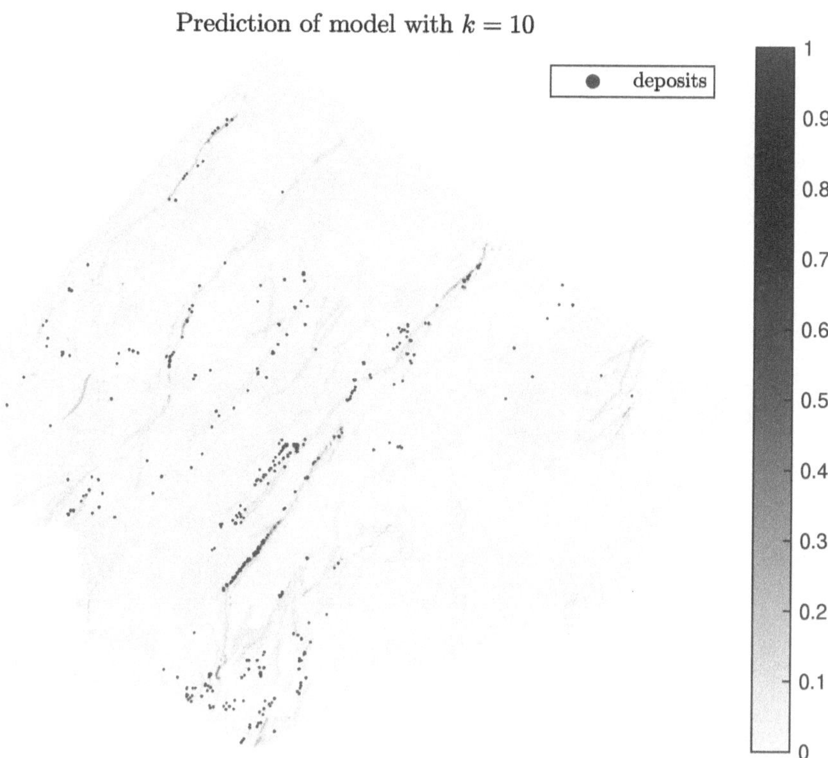

Fig. 7.13.: Model predictions of the model trained with $k = 10$ and the true mineralisations. One can clearly see that the model uncovers some relation between some mineralisations and geological structures. There are lines that indicate the occurrence of mineralisations nearby.

$x7$ and $x8$ is indeed beneficial for gold mineralisations.

7.5.6. Conclusion for the Ghana Dataset

The analysis of the Ghana dataset would justify a work on its own. We applied our model selection method WBIC in different settings and compared it to the model obtained using *stepwiseglm* on sampled data and the neural network. Relying solely on statistical measures, all three methods perform poorly in accurately predicting gold mineralisations. However, there were some structures in the predictions that localize some region in which the occurrence of mineralisations is more likely in all three approaches. Furthermore, using the proposed variations in the labeling of the target and the preselection of negative datapoints, we were able to detect some structures that can be further analyzed by experts. This is possible because the selected model of WBIC is parsimonious, i.e. it selects only a few but important variables. This in turn enables the researcher to focus on these variables and use them for explanation of the underlying truth.

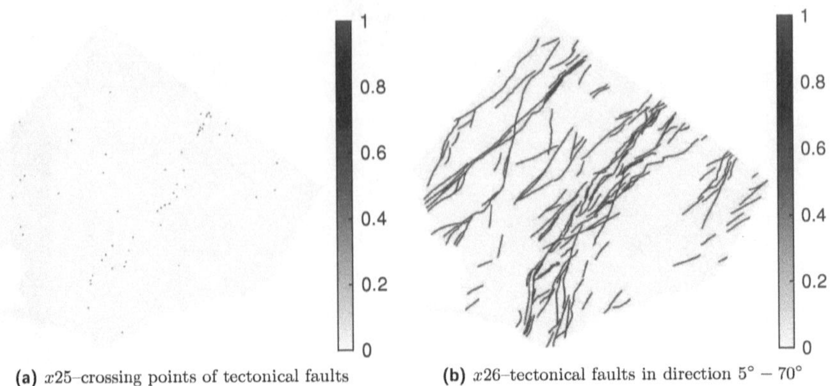

(a) $x25$–crossing points of tectonical faults   **(b)** $x26$–tectonical faults in direction $5° − 70°$

Fig. 7.14.: Variables $x25$ and $x26$ both describing the location and direction of faults.

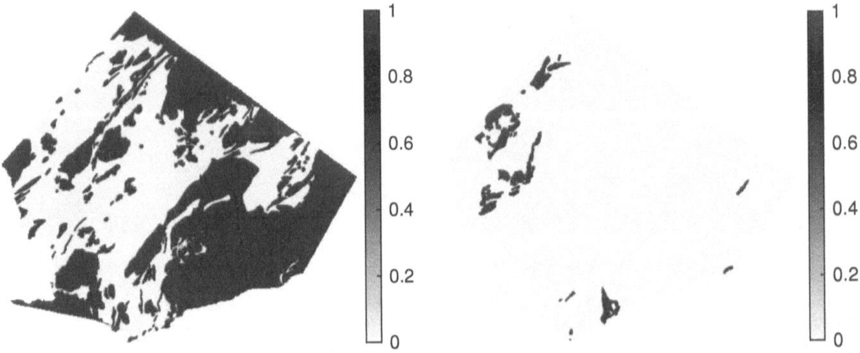

(a) $x1$–unspecified rock type   **(b)** $x7$–interermediate felsic plutonic rock

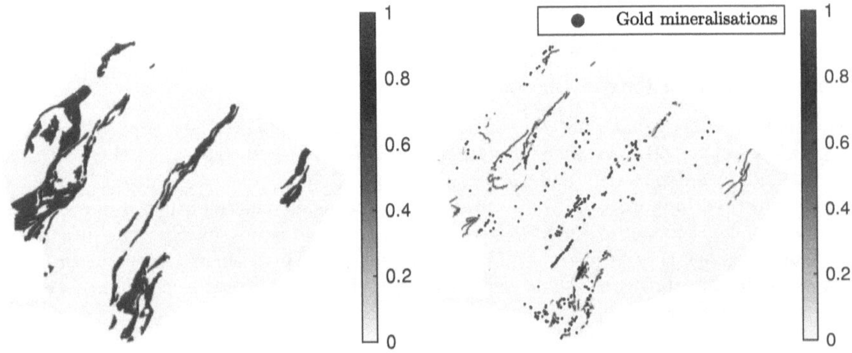

(c) $x8$–mafic volcanic rock   **(d)** Interaction $x1 : x8$ with gold mineralisations

Fig. 7.15.: Variables $x1$ describes the Euclidean distance to a type of rock that is not specified in the data. $x7$ and $x8$ describe the Euclidean distance to intermediate felsic plutonic rock and mafic volcanic rock, respectively. The interaction $x1 : x8$ describes the locations of occurrences of $x1$ and $x8$ which is beneficial for the occurrence of a gold mineralisation.

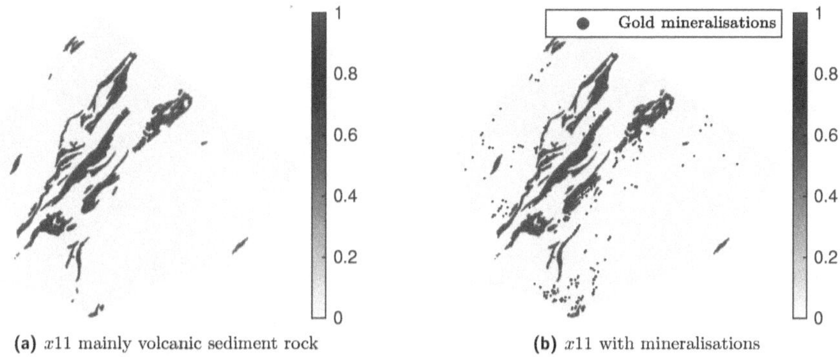

(a) $x11$ mainly volcanic sediment rock

(b) $x11$ with mineralisations

Fig. 7.16.: Variable $x11$ describing the Euclidean distance to a mainly volcanic sediment rock type.

c=5	c=10	c=20	c=40	c=80
Intercept	*Intercept*	*Intercept*	*Intercept*	*Intercept*
$x1$	$x3$	$x3$	$x3$	$x1$
$x3$	$x25$	$x25$	$x10$	$x3$
$x4$	$x26$	$x26$	$x21$	$x25$
$x25$	$x26^2$	$x26^2$	$x25$	$x26$
$x26$	$x1:x3$	$x15:x25$	$x26$	$x26^2$
$x26^2$	$x1:x7$		$x26^2$	
$x1:x3$	$x3:x25$		$x8:x26$	
$x1:x7$	$x4:x9$		$x15:x25$	
$x1:x8$			$x23:x27$	
$x3:x25$				
$x4:x9$				
$x20:x27$				

Tab. 7.19.: Variables that were selected 9 out of 10 runs for different values of c.

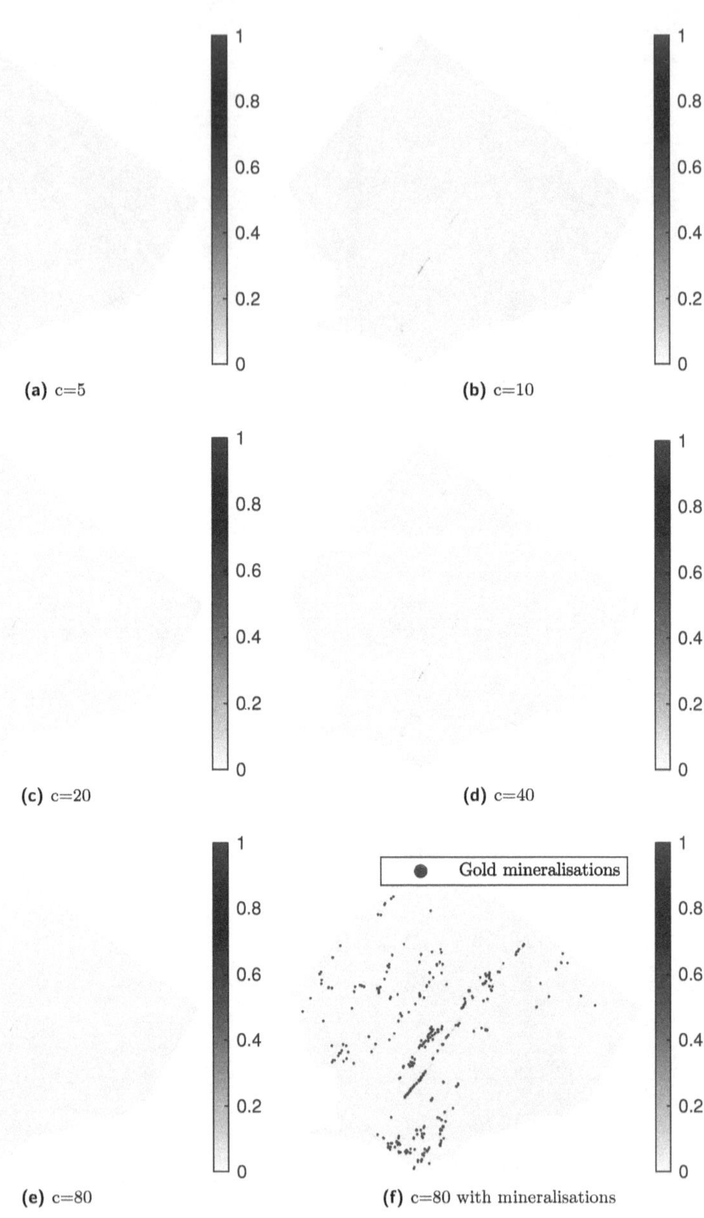

(a) c=5

(b) c=10

(c) c=20

(d) c=40

(e) c=80

(f) c=80 with mineralisations

Fig. 7.17.: Model predictions for different models. Every model was trained on the training area using only negative datapoints that lie in a cluster with at least c positive datapoints.

Part IV.

Conclusion

8. Conclusion

In this book we proposed a new combination of the Wald statistic and the Bayes' information criterion for model selection with logistic regression in the rare event context. This proposed WBIC method takes special care of the fact that the event of interest, i.e. the positive event, is very rare. The applied sampling schemes enables a fast computation which results in a fast model selection process. Furthermore, the obtained models are not only parsimonious but the procedure is quite stable, i.e., the models do not differ largely for different runs. This is very different for the MATLAB function *stepwiseglm*. We developed the final procedure applying several modifications justifying them on two fabricated datasets which simulate a possible dataset from the field of prospectivity modeling. The performance on fabricated data showed the ability of our proposed method to detect a true model or part of the true model that lies inside the model domain.

After proposing the final model selection procedure WBIC it was tested on five real world datasets with rare events including one dataset from prospectivity modeling. Its performance was compared to a neural network and two variants of the *stepwiseglm* function of MATLAB. The experiments showed that WBIC selects models with fewer variables than the stepwise procedure. This enables a better interpretation of the final model which in turn leads to the identification of important variables and interactions. Furthermore, the computation took only a fraction of time of the *stepwiseglm* function. The classification performance was always better than *stepwiseglm* on sampled data and was almost as good as *stepwiseglm* on the whole training data which used many more variables. For the covtype dataset we showed that the classification accuracy can be increased through adding more non-linearities. This results in an increased model selection time and more variables. However, computation time as well as number of selected variables are still smaller than they are with *stepwiseglm* on the full training data.

In addition, we introduced a preselection for negative datapoints using self-organizing-maps. This limits the model selection to mineralisations that are very similar and appear in a relatively large number. It can be used to detect the overall most important features for the largest areas of mineralisations. We have also introduced the technique of the enlargement of the positive target events. This manipulation of the training area introduces some spatial dependency between neighboring datapoints which is otherwise not existent in the data. This uncovers important relationships that are needed for the detection of mineralisations. Hence, the resulting model was able to detect the connection between the distance of the occurrence of some types of rocks and tectonic faults and the occurrence of gold mineralisations.

The results of this book are in preparation for publication in a journal.

9. Future Work

In this book, we have shown a model selection approach for logistic regression in the context of rare events. The resulting models help the researcher and experts comprehend underlying geological structures that might not be known. However, there is still more research to be done.

- Incorporating spatial dependencies between the datapoints is already an ongoing research and some methods have been proposed, i.e. [8, 63, 58]. Applying such methods in combination with our model selection might reveal even more connections.

- The spatial dependency of the data is basically demanding the use of convolutional neural networks. The use of convolutional neural networks for geological settings started recently, i.e. [28, 57]. This should be further developed.

- Since every run of WBIC produces slightly different models one could use model averaging to average the predictions of the different models [16].

- The preselection of negative datapoints using SOM was suggested in this work. This preselection could also be done using other methods such as described in [2, 15].

List of Figures

List of Tables